RENUNCIATION AS A TRAGIC FOCUS

A Study of Five Plays

Act of Renouncing

RENUNCIATION

AS A TRAGIC FOCUS

A Study of Five Plays

by

Eugene H. Falk

WITH AN INTRODUCTION BY
Norman J. DeWitt

University of Minnesota Press, Minneapolis

PUBLISHED IN GREAT BRITAIN, INDIA, AND PAKISTAN BY
GEOFFREY CUMBERLEGE: OXFORD UNIVERSITY PRESS, LONDON, BOMBAY, AND KARACHI

TO

CLARENCE D. L. ROPP

Nil ego contulerim iucundo sanus amico.

HORACE

Acknowledgments

I WISH to express my indebtedness to Professors Norman J. DeWitt, Walter T. Pattison, and Reino Virtanen for reading the manuscript and for their constructive suggestions. I am particularly grateful to Professor DeWitt for the essay, "Tragedy and Personal Humanism," which he has written as an introduction to my work.

Miss Ruth Altmann of the University of Minnesota Press, who was directly responsible for the editorial work, has earned my respect for the tact and understanding she showed in working with my manuscript.

I wish to thank the Cambridge University Press for granting permission to use Sir Richard C. Jebb's translations in *The Tragedies of Sophocles* (1912) for all my quotations from *Oedipus the King, Antigone,* and *Oedipus at Colonus,* and Princeton University Press for consenting to my use of Lacy Lockert's brilliant translation of *Polyeucte* in *The Chief Plays of Corneille* (1952).

I have used my own translations for the quoted passages from *Aglavaine and Selysette* (Maurice Maeterlinck, *Théâtre,* vol. III, Bruxelles: P. Lacomblez, and Paris: Per Lamm, 1901), and also from *Polyphème* (Albert Samain, *Polyphème,* Paris: Société du Mercure de France, 1906).

E. H. F.

Minneapolis, May 1954

Tragedy
and Personal Humanism

by NORMAN J. DeWITT

THIS brief essay, like many other introductions, is actually a post-script. And since it is also a report on one reader's experience, it may well be justified as a warning to other readers. The warning is that the essays which follow have been written in terms of a personal humanism. The reader may find, therefore, that the critical terms employed are not those to which he is accustomed.

The reference to "personal" humanism suggests, of course, that there are kinds of humanism. The reference also implies that personal humanism is a distinct kind, and that it is opposed to, or may be contrasted with, other kinds of humanism which form a completely different general class. For descriptive purposes, we may call the other kinds of humanism *impersonal* or *academic*.

Now that these terms have been recorded, we may consider the possibility that a higher value is to be attached to personal humanism than to the kind we are calling academic or impersonal. In order, therefore, to construe the essays which follow, we shall try to clarify the terms "personal" and "academic," and to see wherein personal humanism differs from academic humanism and wherein, by so differing, a personal humanism has superior value.

First of all, one may say, without inviting controversy, that humanism in academic circles has become extraordinarily confused. For while man is advertised as the interest of the "humanities" at all times, the actual focus of interest seems to rest very frequently upon works of human art.

It is very difficult, therefore, to dissociate aesthetic appreciation from academic humanism and the humanities; and when great ideas are found in the same schedule as selections from the fine arts, one is tempted to conclude that the ideas, too, are selected and displayed for aesthetic rather than for pragmatic reasons. A humanities course may then assume the aspect of a museum; the student is taken on a conducted tour, as it were, and, like the tourist, he is not expected to handle the artifacts, much less take them home. In this context, what we call humanism may become intellectual tourism.

If, on the other hand, we direct our interest toward the humanistic ideal, or the concept of man at his best (what the fifth-century Greek called *areté*), we are likely to find that, under the influence of aesthetics, the artist has somehow become the ultimate ideal of humanism. But since this ideal is unattainable, we readily transfer our attention from the artist to the work of art. The critic then becomes the ideal human, with the inference that aesthetic experience, or organized appreciation, is the end of humanistic education. Unfortunately, however, when we make aesthetic experience the main concern of humanism, we run the risk of confusing Man Feeling with the Emersonian ideal of Man Thinking.

One might then go on to examine the corollary Renaissance tendency to confuse the fine arts with civilization, followed by the tendencies of primitivism and romanticism . . . and so forth. There will be little point, however, in proceeding to an anthology of tendencies when we can simplify our task by indicating that the basic problem of our academic humanism concerns the relationship of the observer to the material of his observation. Here, in fact, is one of the central problems of the intellectual tradition of the West.

The problem may be demonstrated by a very simple example. Much of our knowledge of the preschool child issues from an arrangement whereby the expert observer sits behind a one-way window or screen in the laboratory school. He can see the little people, but they cannot see him. He is therefore in a position to be "objective," whereas, if he were actually one with the little people, sharing their experiences, his observations would be "subjective" and hence of dubious scientific value.

Now, while there may be certain pragmatic advantages in this arrangement from the standpoint of the sciences of human action, it may, at the same time, raise some doubts in the minds of old-fashioned libertarians. In a scientific age, to be sure, very few will share the belief that the circumstances of science may fail to enhance the dignity of the individual on either side of the screen. After all, the personal dignity of a four-year-old is a matter of some uncertainty; and one must assume that the expert observer, in his capacity as expert, is a mere recording device and hence superior to old-fashioned proprieties.

The problem becomes more acute, however, when one elevates the circumstances of the laboratory school to the level of logical, or systematic, or objective, or scientific, observation of human action at large. The one-way screen is still there, in the form of scientific detachment. Or is it? Can the social scientist claim immunity from social "forces"? Or, granted that the one-way screen is effective, can the observer claim immunity from collective academic subjectivity? That is, can he claim to be immune from academic trends, movements, interests, fashions, prejudices — the social forces of his detached community? Can the student of society be both a member of society and not a member of society at the same time? Can objectivity be turned off and on, like a light? Or, may we put the question in an Aristotelian form and conclude that, since the observer of human action is not acting as a human being during his professional periods, he must be either a beast or a god — if not all the time, at least off and on?

Some of the elder German sociologists, who appreciated the principles of scientific caution, worried about the problem of objectivity a good deal; but today, under the spell of the sentimental views of man which play so large a part in the history of our social and behavioral sciences, and convinced by our apparent pragmatic successes, we are not likely to have heard of the problem of objectivity, much less to have worried about it. But the problem of objectivity in relation to the observation of human action remains.

To be sure, we may join Plato in ignoring the whole problem of objectivity in relation to human action. We may simply conclude that the circumstances of the problem are unreal. Reality lies in metaphysical entity, not in human action. We keep the screen, but we try to look in the other direction, away from it. Quite characteristically, modern humanism has embraced some of Plato's metaphysics without embracing the Platonic field of meaning in its entirety. After taking Plato in a survey course and learning to appreciate his ideas, we easily arrive at two concepts of man at his best: the Ph.D. and the artist. The one is a pursuer of truth, the other a pursuer of beauty. But, in Platonic language, truth and beauty are the same thing, to be identified with the highest good, above the realm of common thought and action, beyond the context of the screen. The result is again confusion, especially when we try to decide whether the Ph.D. and the artist, like science and the humanities, are true opposites or merely complements, like the separated lovers in Plato's *Symposium*.

With Aristotle, the one-way screen becomes a permanent part of the academic apparatus. We place a tragic action on the table, like a cat in a zoology course, and subject it to detached critical analysis. Unfortunately, the subject of our dissection quickly expires, provided that it has not done so before we begin. (One might add that there is no trace of fear or pity in the *Poetics*.) But the analogy may be carried even further. The academic method, like the older zoology, must deal with gross structures and finite things which can be viewed, as Aristotle put it, as a whole and in a moment of time: poetry, tragedy, art, knowledge, *the* child, each viewed *in general* or as a *whole*. If the object of study cannot be viewed in this way, in the mind's eye, as it were, it must be reduced to the necessary proportions. Beyond this, to explore the difficulties which the academic method then entails in terms of empirical procedures would require more space than can be claimed here. We must be content with the statement that human thought and action in time are very difficult things to deal with academically because they are not things at all in the academic sense.

For all of this, every student of literature should know the *Poetics* virtually by heart. They show a very great scholar at work, in the best Emersonian sense. The master's incidental remarks should be treated with very great respect. The *Poetics* also demonstrate the standard procedures of academic detachment; e.g., the historical and comparative methods, the determination of an end or goal, classification, analysis, reduction to the unique, and, most important, generalization or reduction to organic unity. In these procedures we find a demonstration of the major premise of the academic tradition: man is by nature a rational being in a rational universe in which all things are subject to rational analysis. Reason is both natural and nature itself. And the essential condition of reason is objectivity or critical detachment — without fear or pity.

Thus, in the academic tradition, we have constructed a set of either-or's, or opposites, which we take to be derived from reality. Judgments must be either subjective or objective. Man is either rational or irrational. Things are either subject to rational analysis, or they are not subject to understanding at all. If things are irrational — i.e., the universe — and if man is one with the universe (and we would like to think that he is), then man must be irrational. Our academic value system is constructed around these inescapable alternatives. Yet, in the modern world, the old value system seems to be of rather dubious empirical validity. Caught, as we are, between a traditional value system and its apparent denial by real experience, we are terribly confused. Indeed, if we may borrow a term from the field of electronic communications, the original signal, whatever it may be, is completely drowned out by "noise."

The noise, and confusion, and the uncertainty of the signal, have led many to conclude, quite logically, that the situation is hopeless for the rational man. This conclusion has contributed to the continental movements of despair which we have heard of from abroad. Anglo-American humanists, who, fortunately in this instance at least, are neither empiricists nor strict logicians, are able to view systematic despair with interest, but with academic detachment — thus adding to their own repertoire of confusion. The continentals, given to clearer thinking, have seen the dilemma but cannot solve it by logic — because there is no logical solution. Man is either rational or irrational. Modern experience suggests that reason cannot cope with either man or things; hence man and things are irrational. With that conclusion, the Western system of values seems to crumble into existentialism abroad and into panel discussions at home.

But we have forgotten something. We have forgotten the massive empirical and pragmatic tradition of the West, which leads to another kind of humanism. We have forgotten, too, that the great ideas do not necessarily have aesthetic appeal, nor are they necessarily written up with stylistic charm in the great books. Moreover, as the classical pragmatist, Epicurus, pointed out, logic is not an instrument for the discovery of truth. Experience in, and as part of, this world, is the source and test of truth; and logical dilemmas, one may add, may be so simple as to be false. When we say that man is either rational or irrational, objective or subjective, controlled either by reason or emotion, we may not be making a significant statement at all. The right answer may not be subject to expression in terms of *either-or*; the right answer may be neither. And that may be how the great things are. The great things may be neither rational nor irrational. They may be superrational; and man's great and unique instrument may be hyperlogic.

Thus the universe is being explored today by men who combine strict empiricism with conceptual brilliance, heirs of the classical empiricists whom the academic humanist has rejected since Plato's day. Today, as then, true science goes beyond academic logic. And we, if we wish, as true humanists, may claim the heritage of the forgotten pragmatic and empirical humanism of the West, which, in its own way, went beyond logic, intellectual mechanics, and determinism, and has been equally rejected by academic humanism from Plato's day to this. We are faced

with the possibility, then, that the academic tradition has sys-
tematically underrated man, and that, when translated into education, it forces the specific individual to a lower status than is his
right in, and by, nature.

Here, perhaps, lie the directions of a new humanism that is also
a very old one.

The new directions lead us back into an old world in which
there are no one-way screens. The standards of judgment are
personal experience in the real world of human action in space
and time. But what would otherwise appear to be subjectivity
(in the academic sense) is subject to strict controls. Our judgments are tempered, sobered, and controlled by fear and pity, by
memories of mishaps, even pain, in our own experience, extended
by our sense of time and our awareness that others, like ourselves,
may be hurt. *Dolemus; ergo sumus.*

Personal humanism comes, then, from an awareness of a world
in which pain is real; and it leads to the traditional virtues of
wisdom and justice, terms that are seldom heard in academic
circles today. In its best and most sensitive form, personal humanism recognizes mental anguish: the conflicts and frustrations of
events and great duties and intentions. Its ideal is simply man at
his best, but not perfect, as we know him in common experience
and as we might be ourselves.

Now, of course, the end of education is action, and action is
better learned by specific examples than by detached academic
generalities. A discussion of academic generalities is always re-
freshed, and sometimes brought to an embarrassing conclusion, by
the asking for and giving of specific examples. We say a great
deal about our faith in the dignity of the individual, but one seldom finds, in support of these professions, a return to experience
through examples of real human dignity — that is, to examples of
real human beings, with an address in time and space, actually
behaving in ways that show us good and great men in action.

As personal humanists, then, let us proceed at once to specific
cases of human experience. In the studies that follow, we may
look at human beings who have been made more real, and some-

times larger, than life by dramatic art. It will be the responsibility of the critic to examine human experience that may differ from our own in degree but not in kind or quality. If we cannot sense this community of experience, and through it extend our own experience and control our judgments, the fault will not be altogether the critic's.

So much, then, for the warning to the reader, save one remark. Personal humanism places a great responsibility upon the critic, who must also be a teacher. And it calls for courage. The critic cannot claim detachment behind the one-way screen. He must lead his students into the real world where human beings have always lived, in time and space. As a teacher, he must then reveal his own humanity — and to do this, as Quintilian might have said, he must be a *vir bonus peritus docendi* — above all, a good man.

Table of Contents

RENUNCIATION AS A TRAGIC FOCUS

A Study of Five Plays

Can Martyrdom Be Tragic?

"TRAGEDY, in its pure idea, shows us a mortal will engaged in an unequal struggle with destiny, whether that destiny be represented by the forces within or without the mind. The conflict reaches its tragic issue when the individual perishes, but through his ruin the disturbed order of the world is restored and the moral forces reassert their sway." * There is no reason to question the validity of Butcher's definition, although its underlying assumption does seem to limit the scope of dramatic situations which might well fall within the concept of tragedy.

That definition presupposes a tragic character who challenges his destiny in a struggle which proves to be unequal but does not appear so to begin with. It is clear that a tragic flaw in the character and tragic irony in the situation naturally follow from this concept. The tragic issue, the defeat of the individual, leads to the realization that human presumption to determine one's own destiny is necessarily ruinous.

Essentially, the represented tragic experience leads to a keen awareness of human limitations, which imposes humility and awe upon man who is faced with a destiny that to him appears as the unyielding guardian of the order of the world.

It is, however, possible to enlarge this basic concept of tragedy. It will be seen how that definition excludes martyrdom or self-

* S. H. Butcher, *Aristotle's Theory of Poetry and Fine Arts*, 4th ed., 1951 ($4.50), pp. 311–312. Quoted by permission of Dover Publications, Inc., New York 10, N. Y.

3

sacrifice from the realm of the tragic because "the death of the martyr presents to us not the defeat, but the victory of the individual; the issue of a conflict in which the individual is ranged on the same side as the higher powers, and the sense of suffering consequently lost in that of moral triumph." Obviously, if a character, thirsty for a glorious death, rushes to what may prove to be his ruin as cheerfully and single-mindedly as does Corneille's Horace, the sense of suffering is lost and the experience is not tragic for the very reasons cited in the quoted passage.

Yet, in martyrdom and self-sacrifice the character may, though "ranged on the same side as the higher powers," experience suffering in spite, or rather because, of his moral triumph. He may not seek glory in his self-sacrificial act at all, or at least he may not seek it without at the same time experiencing suffering and distress over the self-imposed defeat of his will to live, over the loss of things deeply cherished in life. He may choose self-sacrifice in order to fulfill what he considers to be his duty — a duty which an accepted and respected view of life has imposed upon him; but he may at the same time be keenly aware of the loss of worldly happiness and life, to which his "mortal will" aspires, and which he must renounce to fulfill his duty.

His concept of duty, his spiritual values, may well be equated with what S. H. Butcher calls the "higher powers" or "destiny"; and the "mortal will" to cling to the good life, to the joys and happiness of living, may well be engaged in an "unequal struggle" with a dictate of conscience; a dictate which assumes the functions of destiny as the struggle develops, as the consequences of a persistent adherence to life and happiness appear to the character increasingly unworthy and humiliating in the light of a growing awareness of his spiritual aspirations. The "mortal will" to live, then, does suffer defeat in a distressing and keenly felt act of renunciation. The conflict reaches its tragic issue with the act of renunciation which culminates in self-sacrifice.

Renunciation is, therefore, the criterion by which martyrdom and self-sacrifice can be judged to be tragic or not. The tragic character's suffering and distress, caused by renunciation, measure the intensity of the conflict between his will to live and his devotion to immutable spiritual aspirations demanding self-sacrifice. If he were to conceive matter as the cause of all evil, if he were therefore to deny himself bodily satisfactions and regard them as sinful, if in the vehemence of asceticism he were to fulfill serenely a particular ethical principle, then there would be no conflict, no renunciation, no suffering, and no sacrifice. Similarly, there is no renunciation or self-sacrifice when all the value of life is irredeemably lost and death is nothing more than a form of escape. Martyrdom, without the suffering of renunciation, is not a self-sacrificial act either, when it is sought as a privilege, when it is conceived as a means of personal redemption or self-glorification. The real test for sacrificial martyrdom lies in the firmness of the martyr's positive attitude toward life and in his devotion to what he regards as a supreme value. These are the forces that determine the intensity of the conflict, which to be tragic must be resolved by an act of renunciation that ends in self-sacrifice.

Renunciation is, then, a decision by which the will to live is made to yield to spiritual aspirations recognized to be superior. Renunciation is a tragic experience *for a character* if, in the course of the conflict, the defeat of his will to live by his spiritual aspirations comes to appear inevitable; thereby his spiritual aspirations become his destiny. Furthermore, renunciation is experienced as tragic by the character if the defeat is the cause of suffering and distress.

Renunciation has, *for us*, the effect of being tragic because it evokes our pity for man thus engaged in a distressing struggle to subordinate his will to live to his spiritual aspirations; because a drama in which spiritual aspirations are shown to elicit man's loyalty and devotion fills us with awe; and because we fear, while the decision to renounce evolves in the conflict, that the character may weaken in his determination to uphold his spiritual values, yield to his will to live, destroy his soul, lose our pity, and deprive us of our awe.

Because the intensity of the represented tragic experience of renunciation depends, as we have seen, on the keenness of the struggle between the tragic character's will to live and his spiritual aspirations, the ultimate measure of that intensity is the authenticity of the forces in conflict; for renunciation to be a tragic experience the character's devotion to both worldly and spiritual aspirations must be genuine.

To show this dependence I have chosen five plays in which the tragic experiences are of decreasing intensity. In Sophocles' *Oedipus the King* and *Antigone*, the worldly aspirations of the tragic characters are real — that is, capable of fulfillment — and their devotion to the good life, their will to live, is therefore genuine. At the same time they represent the most authentic devotion to spiritual aspirations, which impose renunciation and self-sacrifice on Oedipus, and renunciation and sacrificial martyrdom on Antigone. When Corneille's *Polyeucte* is compared with the plays of Sophocles, the worldly aspirations appear less certain of realization and the will to live therefore less genuine. The accepted superior values, however sincerely adhered to, appear to be forced on the character by circumstance. In Maeterlinck's *Aglavaine and Selysette*, the will to live is even more diminished and the spiritual aspiration is forced on the tragic character without ever eliciting an adherence out of conviction. Finally, in Samain's *Polyphème*, the happiness the character seeks in life is clearly beyond any hope of ever being realized and the spiritual aspiration only appears as an afterthought to the character's self-sacrificial act. These plays represent a progression from authentic to seeming renunciation.

Oedipus the King

THE skepticism of Protagoras, a somewhat younger contemporary of Sophocles, has not penetrated *Oedipus the King*. In *Antigone*, the skeptic view of life seems to be represented by Creon, and with him it is destined for defeat. Man is not yet the measure of all things, as the great Sophist of Abdera thought he was; the course of his life is still dependent on the will of the gods. Man is not yet the master of his destiny, and his success is not yet the effect of his wisdom or cunning. Fate is not a blind irrational force, nor does man, in blind devotion to deity, throw himself under the wheels of a Juggernaut. Man obeys a respected law, and fate, however mysterious, is not without purpose.

Oedipus feels that his fate is governed by a superior power, which imposes responsibilities on him, and he knows that he must fulfill his duties and recognize them as his. Such is Oedipus who faces the men of Thebes. They stand as suppliants before the palace of their king. A terrible plague is ravaging the city, and Oedipus, "the king glorious in all eyes," the "saviour," is being beseeched to save his people as he did before when the Sphinx was spreading terror over the land.

Oedipus, the "first of men," is well aware of the people's suffering and his "soul mourns" for his city as well as for himself. He is not merely a king pitying his people, and this is not merely compassion; this is immediate suffering caused by the pain in

7

his own body, by the grief and anguish in his own heart; for the king and his city are *one*. This oneness, which characterizes the relationship of all in the city, is the very foundation of this tragedy and of its meaning.

Great is the king's despair, and in his helplessness he shows humility: ". . . be sure that I have wept full many tears, gone many ways in wanderings of thought. And the sole remedy which, well pondering, I could find . . ." was to send Creon to seek Apollo's advice. It seems that Oedipus wishes to emphasize the importance of the man he has chosen for this vital mission: "I have sent the son of Menoeceus, Creon, mine own wife's brother . . ." It can be assumed that Creon has been chosen because of his rank and, apparently, not without fear on the part of Oedipus. This point needs to be stressed, for it leads to a fuller appreciation of the action itself.

Creon is late in returning from Delphi with the divine message and Oedipus laments before his people: ". . . it troubles me what he doth; for he tarries strangely, beyond the fitting space." This is a statement of considerable significance and not a mere record of transient feelings. This is the first hint at a nascent suspicion. We do not know yet why such a "lapse of days" is of great concern to Oedipus, and not until the blind seer Tiresias appears do we perceive the significance of these allusions.

Creon's arrival and his exalted announcement that he is the bearer of "good news" do not seem to dispel Oedipus' suspicion: "But what is the oracle? So far, thy words make me neither bold nor yet afraid." Instead of accepting Creon's words as a joyful signal for general jubilation, as a source of spiritual relief from the anguish which was made even more acute by Creon's tarrying, Oedipus considers Creon's good news as a possible threat and, therefore, as a cause for fear. Creon's triumphant mood and confidence make Oedipus even more aware of his own nascent distrust. As if driven by fear to secure his position, Oedipus reaffirms his identity with his people, his oneness with them, and above all his responsibility and devotion: "Speak before all: the sorrow which I bear is for those more than for mine own life." It is obvious that Oedipus fears and expects a message that will bring sorrow. Thereupon Creon proclaims the will of the god. They shall "drive out a defiling thing." The death of the late king, Laius, has not been avenged and the plague is caused by the presence of that defiling thing in the midst of the city. Banishment or "bloodshed in quittance of bloodshed" will cleanse the city.

It is noteworthy that both the plague and this oracle, as just reported by Creon, are known to be Sophocles' own contributions to the Oedipus myth. These contributions are essential dramatic factors in the play. Though the two are interwoven, the oracle is the one that develops Oedipus' suspicion of Creon's motives, thus becoming the cause of his own self-deception. The plague, on the other hand, has a dual function; it is the constant background and setting of the play, and also the origin of its tragic course. Because the plague is placed in this focal position, we may assume that Sophocles and his audience believed that a plague can be brought upon a community by a "defiling thing," by a sinner who lives in its midst. We may also assume that they considered the plague as a punishment imposed by the gods, and consequently believed that the innocent suffer justly with the guilty, as Heinrich Weinstock has pointed out in his memorable *Sophokles.**

While using the plague in that focal position, Sophocles also stressed that Oedipus, that defiling thing which is causing the plague to ravage Thebes, killed his father not only in self-defense, but without the slightest knowledge of Laius' identity. Oedipus committed a murder on a stranger and in self-defense, an act which was not considered sinful. In this connection it is worth while to remember Oedipus' own meditation in *Oedipus at Colonus*:

And yet in nature how was I evil? I, who was but requiting a wrong, so that, had I been acting with knowledge, even then I could not be accounted wicked; but, as it was, all unknowing went I — whither I went . . .

* Wuppertal: Marées-Verlag, 1948.

9

And yet he must have been guilty in the eyes of the gods, and evidently, in all his innocence, he considered himself guilty too. In his innocence he was made an agent of sin and condemned to cause suffering and to suffer. Though he suffered willingly, it was not without self-pity. Whose guilt could it have been then that caused him to suffer, though "he could not be accounted wicked"? If his unintentional deeds caused his innocent people to suffer, whose guilt "brought the tempest" upon him?

The curse of Pelops hurled against Laius, who had sinned against his gracious host's son, was common knowledge. The oracle that forbade Laius to have children and the prophecy that he would be killed by his own son, should he disobey the order, were equally well known. It was Laius who had sinned, it was he who had failed to atone for his sin by sacrificing the happiness of fatherhood, by self-denial. It was this sinful omission that caused Oedipus to be born and to fulfill the ordered punishment of his father, to become an instrument of punishment with the inevitability of becoming the unsuspecting agent of crime and sin. This is what the play itself expresses in the course of the plot, and what must be understood if the chosen focus, the expressly introduced plague, is to have any meaning at all. To suggest that the play portrays the cruelty of irrational evil, or the mere humiliation of man by the gods, is to completely disregard Oedipus' own testimony of his guilt, however different its meaning may be from the one it has acquired in our own civilization. To interpret the play in this way means to disregard the deep meaning of Oedipus' self-imposed punishment, without which the play could not convey the tragic content that it does.

We shall, then, have to answer the question of why Oedipus feels guilty — guilty in a special sense — in spite of his innocence. Such an answer will explain his conception of justice, his concern for the rites of cleansing, his acts of atonement, his self-sacrifice and self-pity, his bonds with gods and men.

Just as the plague symbolizes moral interdependence in space, which embraces those who share a common life in a given area, it also presumes moral interdependence in time. It shows that Oedipus is guilty and that for his guilt Thebes suffers. Since he himself acted without sinful intentions, his guilt cannot originate in him. His sinful acts were brought about by Laius' own sin and, of course, by Jocasta's as well. Sinful acts are his inheritance, which parental guilt has passed on to the son, and it is because of their guilt that Oedipus suffers. This is the basis of the oracle that drove him away from Corinth. That oracle is linked to the guilt of the parents. To separate the basis of that oracle from the focal point of the play and to isolate the plague from all its implications, to place the play in a vacuum and to ascribe all the important events to the whim of the gods, or to Oedipus' tragic flaw, is to limit the scope of the play and to misplace its emphasis.

Thebes suffers because of Oedipus, and Oedipus suffers because of Laius. Since the play is based on the concept of oneness, the associated concepts of transferred guilt and inherited guilt are fundamental elements of this tragedy.

The very thought of trying to find a moral justification for these concepts shocks our sense of justice, and we are tempted to stamp the deep belief in the justice of these concepts as blind devotion to a fearful deity. We like to think of ourselves as being endowed with individuality, with the power to determine our own course of action according to values freely chosen, or at least freely adhered to. We are willing to assume responsibility for any action, but we object to being blamed for the misdeeds of others, even if they are our kinsmen. We like to be esteemed for our own virtues and are willing to be punished for our own sins. In the matter of morals and social acceptability we demand that we be judged as unrelated individuals. We even go so far as to demand that only our own immediate past be taken into consideration when moral judgment is passed on us. Our stress on individuality is the result of our emancipation from original social ties, whose meaning has been gradually lost as man's capacity for independent living has increased.

The belief in transferred or inherited guilt belongs to an era of strong family ties and clan loyalties. It belongs to an era in which these ties and loyalties cause man's actions and their effects to be closely observed and measured, in which there is a strong belief that no man's actions can stand isolated and that all he does may affect not only himself, but others too; he is, therefore, not only responsible to himself, but also to those affected by his deeds. No one can live or die for himself alone when there is an intense awareness of one's family and clan responsibility. Furthermore, this concept of transferred and inherited guilt imposes on man an even graver responsibility, for it belongs to an era in which deity is not only the guardian of law and the possessor of the light of foresight, but also the representative of eternal life. Man is not only reminded of his responsibilities during his ephemeral earthly existence but also of those imposed by his belief in the reality of a beyond. (One of the reasons Oedipus gives for blinding himself is his fear of his parents' gaze when he will meet them in Hades.) Man cannot live for the present alone, since life on earth is but a stage in the flow of eternity.

In the light of these beliefs the concept of inherited and transferred guilt does not appear unjust. It is just, when loyalties outlast earthly life, when one generation after the other carries the same torch of life just as all living men have their share in the one life, when life is *one*. Life is an inheritance which we receive with all its liabilities. We are only innocent insofar as we do not intentionally and knowingly increase the liabilities before we pass on our share of life to our progeny. Guilt, if incurred by a progenitor clings to our inherited life as long as cleansing and atonement do not free it from its blemish. As long as man desires to live the share of life he has inherited, he has to accept it with all its demands and obligations and he has to guard it as a trust for posterity.

Man's primary obligation is to life itself, for life is divine. It is his obligation to make it pure, to keep it pure, and to transmit it pure. If he fails in this obligation, he is guilty and imposes the burden of guilt on his children. But if he does try to fulfill his obligation, if he does try to avoid personal guilt, and if in spite of his best intentions he finds that involuntary defilement has been the result of his endeavors, it is then that he learns of his inherited guilt, or of his transferred guilt, of his debt and thus of his unworthiness. This is the realization which makes Oedipus exclaim: "For now I am found evil, and of evil birth . . ." or ". . . lead me hence, the utterly lost, the thrice accursed, yea, the mortal most abhorred of heaven!"

Oedipus learns that man errs as the result of justice taking its course and that destiny follows justice rather than kindness. He learns that sinning where there is every desire not to sin, and inflicting suffering on others where there is every desire to shield them from it, are marks of disgrace and unworthiness, reminders of sins that cling to one's life and demand retribution and atonement.

That is the concept of life which emerges from the play. According to this concept, life is entrusted to man by the gods; man holds this trust in common with his fellow men, is responsible to them and to the gods for keeping it free of defilement, and is aware of his obligation to relinquish his share of it cleansed and pure. Here innocence is individual, but guilt is shared and perpetuated, for it clings to one's share of life. Thus, retribution is just, since life is one and only its ephemeral human manifestations vary. The individual has duties and his claim to happiness is subject to their observance. If it is his lot to inherit a polluted share of life, he may and does bewail his fate, indulge in self-pity, and resent the irresponsibility of his ancestors who failed in their obligation to keep their share of life pure. He is guilty as long as his life remains uncleansed. If it is his lot to share his life with men who defile it, it is his duty to find the cause of pollution and to remove it or destroy it. He is guilty as long as he has not cast out the defiling element. This is the meaning of the oracle.

It has been quite customary to point out Oedipus' dullness, even blindness, when he finds himself confronted with the growing evidence of his guilt. There are, however, several good

13

reasons which justify his attitude and give it a very different meaning. To understand it, it is necessary to recognize first of all that as long as the last crushing evidence was not yet uncovered, Oedipus really believed himself to be the son of Polybus and Meropè:

> At a banquet, a man full of wine cast it at me in his cups that I was not the true son of my sire . . . but on the next [day] I went to my mother and father, and questioned them; and they were wroth for the taunt with him who had let that word fly. So on their part I had comfort; yet was this thing ever rankling in my heart; for it still crept abroad with strong rumour. And, unknown to mother or father, I went to Delphi; and Phoebus sent me forth disappointed of that knowledge for which I came, but in his response set forth other things, full of sorrow and terror and woe; even that I was fated to defile my mother's bed; and that I should show unto men a brood which they could not endure to behold; and that I should be the slayer of the sire who begat me.
>
> And I, when I listened to this, turned to flight from the land of Corinth, thenceforth wotting of its region by the stars alone, to some spot where I should never see fulfillment of the infamies foretold in mine evil doom.

It is clear that he interpreted the warning of the god as signifying that he would sin against Polybus and Merope, especially since his question to the god was left unanswered; and he had therefore every reason to assume that his question deserved no further attention. Also he had been reassured by Polybus and Meropè, whom he had no reason to distrust, and the insult was hurled at him by a "man full of wine."

It seems that Oedipus kept this oracle very secret. Not even Jocasta was allowed to know that the oracle had marked him as a cursed man, as is evident from what he told her prior to the just quoted confession:

> Yea, and it shall not be kept from thee, now that my forebodings have advanced so far. Who, indeed, is more to me than thou, to whom I should speak in passing through such a fortune as this?

14

He chose Creon, who was his peer in the kingdom, for a mission which, considering his secret, was of some danger to his own reputation. It can now be understood why Creon's prolonged absence has filled Oedipus with apprehension. And, furthermore, was not Creon the regent in Thebes at the time of the Sphinx? Did he not have to yield his power to Oedipus, who saved the city from the monster? Creon seems to him a potential rival and Oedipus suspects him of wishing to use such damaging knowledge about the king to his own advantage.

Creon, completely unaware of Oedipus' fears, is anxious to provide whatever clues he has about the murder of Laius, but Oedipus' suspicion increases the more he learns about the fate of the late king. Oedipus does not expect Creon to try to accuse him of the murder of Laius, since Creon speaks of robbers: ". . . robbers met and fell on them, not in one man's might, but with full many hands." He does, however, expect him to make use of whatever knowledge he has acquired concerning the curse on Oedipus. His suspicion of Creon's intentions drives him to link the robbers with Creon's scheming:

OEDIPUS

How, then, unless there was some trafficking in bribes from here, should the robber have dared thus far?

CREON

Such things were surmised; but, Laïus once slain, amid our troubles no avenger arose.

OEDIPUS

But, when royalty had fallen thus, what trouble in your path can have hindered a full search?

CREON

The riddling Sphinx had made us let dark things go, and was inviting us to think of what lay at our doors.

To Oedipus, Creon's guilt now seems certain, and he feels that it is up to himself to find the slayer:

. . . ye shall find me too leagued with you in seeking vengeance for this land, and for the god besides. On behalf of no far-off friend, no, but in mine own cause, shall I dispel this taint. For whoever was the slayer of Laïus might wish to take vengeance on me also with a hand as fierce. Therefore, in doing right to Laïus, I serve myself.

It is in this state of mind that Oedipus will approach Tiresias. He will try to win him, to enlist his help in finding the culprit, and to uncover Creon's crime:

. . . great prophet, we find in thee our protector and only saviour . . . Do thou, then, grudge neither voice of birds nor any other way of seer-lore that thou hast, but rescue thyself and the State, rescue me, rescue all that is defiled by the dead . . .

The fear of being exposed as an accursed man and of losing power, and the suspicion that Creon may have removed Laius and would now wish to ascend the throne himself, are the powerful motives that prevent Oedipus from recognizing any evidence of guilt that may condemn himself. He cannot, therefore, appreciate the seer's benevolent silence. If Tiresias is not willing to speak, if he is not willing to disclose the identity of the slayer, Oedipus suspects that it must be because of the seer's desire to shield Creon. Also, if Tiresias knows the culprit, he must be guilty himself:

Know that thou seemest to me e'en to have helped in plotting the deed, and to have done it, short of slaying with thy hands. Hadst thou eyesight, I would have said that the doing, also, of this thing was thine alone.

Provoked, Tiresias hurls the accusation of murder and incest against Oedipus, though, moved by pity, he is anxious to spare him. Oedipus should not be considered dull-witted for not taking Tiresias seriously. After all, the seer does exactly what Oedipus has already expected Creon to do: expose the curse. It begins to seem clear to him now why Creon has advised him to seek Tiresias' counsel. However, he has not expected to find himself actually identified with the slayer of Laius. This direct assault on his person not only confirms his suspicion of the former regent, but also makes him realize the seriousness of Creon's conspiracy and the necessity of an immediate investigation of all available clues.

Obviously, Oedipus is not too greatly impressed with Tiresias' power as a seer, but the seer's prestige in Thebes would have been valuable to him if he had been willing to provide the needed testimony against Creon. That explains Oedipus' rather obsequious attitude at the beginning of the scene. Oedipus believes that he is about to uncover Creon's plot against Laius and himself, and this belief prevents him from attributing any credence to Tiresias' accusation, especially since this accusation constitutes, in his own mind, the very proof of the plotting. In any case, Oedipus could in no way have had faith in Tiresias' art as a seer after he had displayed such signal incompetence when the Sphinx was threatening the lives of the city:

O wealth, and empire, and skill surpassing skill in life's keen rivalries, how great is the envy that cleaves to you, if for the sake, yea, of this power which the city hath put into my hands, a gift unsought, Creon the trusty, Creon mine old friend, hath crept on me by stealth, yearning to thrust me out of it, and hath suborned such a scheming juggler as this, a tricky quack, who hath eyes only for his gains, but in his art is blind!

Come, now, tell me, where hast thou proved thyself a seer? Why, when the Watcher was here who wove dark song, didst thou say nothing that could free this folk? Yet the riddle, at least, was not for the first comer to read; there was need of a seer's skill; and none such thou wast found to have, either by help of birds, or as known from any god: no, I came, I, Oedipus the ignorant, and made her mute, when I had seized the answer by my wit, untaught of birds. And it is I whom thou art trying to oust, thinking to stand close to Creon's throne.

Oedipus finds added proof for suspecting Tiresias in the fact that the seer kept silent about the murderer at the time of Laius' death. Nor did Tiresias see any reason to accuse Oedipus when he ascended the throne after delivering Thebes from the Sphinx. For Oedipus one thing seems clear: while Creon was in Delphi he found out about the curse and now feels secure enough in his possession of so damaging a piece of information concerning the king to attempt to overthrow him by accusing him of Laius' murder, using Tiresias for his purpose. In vain are Creon's sincere protestations of innocence, in vain does he try to allay Oedipus' unjustified suspicions:

And, in proof of this, first, go to Pytho, and ask if I brought thee true word of the oracle; then next, if thou find that I have planned aught in concert with the soothsayer, take and slay me, by the sentence not of one mouth, but of twain — by mine own, no less than thine. But make me not guilty in a corner, on unproved surmise . . .

All the evidence seems to condemn Creon in Oedipus' mind. This not only determines the direction of his thinking, but it also precipitates the action:

When the stealthy plotter is moving on me in quick sort, I, too, must be quick with my counterplot. If I await him in repose, his ends will have been gained, and mine missed.

Oedipus decides that Creon must die: ". . . that thou mayest show forth what manner of thing is envy."

Creon's eloquent self-defense does not cause Oedipus to change his mind. And yet, in spite of his unshaken conviction of Creon's guilt, Oedipus does yield to the wishes of the men of Thebes who try to save Creon because he has resorted to a curse and has thereby convinced them of his innocence: "Now may I see no good, but perish accursed, if I have done aught to thee of that wherewith thou chargest me!" Immediately, Jocasta pleads with Oedipus:

O, for the gods' love, believe it, Oedipus — first, for the awful sake of this oath unto the gods, — then for my sake and for theirs who stand before thee.

The Thebans, too, come to Creon's aid:

Respect him who aforetime was not foolish, and who now is strong in his oath . . . thou shouldest never use an unproved rumour to cast a dishonouring charge on the friend who has bound himself with a curse.

In their eyes Creon's innocence is now fully established and he stands vindicated beyond any doubt.

A curse carries weight for, according to popular belief, curses lead to their fulfillment, and Oedipus has every reason to keep his own curse a dark secret and to fear the consequences its revelation to the city might have. However, the Chorus assures Oedipus with an equally strong oath that Creon's innocence in no way establishes his guilt, in spite of Tiresias' accusations. Yet Oedipus knows that if Creon is cleared of all suspicion, he himself is "surely doomed to death, or to be thrust dishonoured from the land . . ."

At this point the emphasis and the motivation of the action change. Oedipus is no longer trying to find added evidence to prove Creon's guilt. From now on, he must try to establish his own innocence. Whereas before he was anxious to prove Creon's guilt, primarily to save his own power and to rid his city of the plague by avenging Laius' death, he will now want to prove to himself — particularly to himself, since the Chorus has assured him of Thebes' confidence — his innocence of the slaying of Laius. It is, after all, this murder which has caused the plague and the suffering. Up to this point, Oedipus has fought to save his crown and his people. From now on, he must save his conscience. By turning his suspicions against himself, he may yet save Thebes again, he may once more unravel the mystery and drive the curse from the land, but this time he is the Sphinx-like monster himself.

Urged by Jocasta, Oedipus tells her: "He [Creon] says that I stand guilty of the blood of Laïus . . . he hath made a rascal seer his mouthpiece; as for himself, he keeps his lips wholly pure." Oedipus reports only that part of Tiresias' accusation which, to his own mind, could possibly apply to him. He easily dismisses the other accusations since he believes that this knowledge of the curse with whose fulfillment he is threatened has been imparted to Tiresias by Creon. But the slaying itself he does not dismiss, for he did kill, in self-defense, prior to his arrival in Thebes. This, too, he has kept a secret and he is now afraid that the man he killed may have been Laius. This fear, foremost in his mind, forces him to turn a suspecting eye upon himself, not, however, to clear himself in the eyes of the Thebans, for they have assured him of their belief in his innocence and he is no longer afraid of losing his power. His perseverance in the search, the desire to know whether it is he who killed the man whom he succeeded on the throne — these are at the dictate of his conscience and of his fear that he may have caused the plague:

But if this stranger had any tie of kinship* with Laïus, who is now more wretched than the man before thee? What mortal could prove more hated of heaven? Whom no stranger, no citizen, is allowed to receive in his house; whom it is unlawful that any one accost; whom all must repel from their homes! And this — this curse — was laid on me by no mouth but mine own!

This is the fear of the outcast, the fear of the marked man whom the gods have caused to sin because he is hateful in their eyes, hateful in spite of his innocence. Can he not clear himself in his own conscience? Did he not act in self-defense? Was the evil deed not forced on him? Should the curse he had hurled against the slayer of Laius fall on him too, on him who committed a sinful act without any sinful intent? And his conscience makes him say: "And I pollute the bed of the slain man with the hands by which he perished. Say, am I vile? Oh, am I not utterly unclean?" Oedipus does not feel free to plead innocence. How could he be innocent if he is "hated of heaven"? His guilt must then precede his sinful act and the sinful act must be a punishment to him whose one desire was to remain clean. And if he should already have sinned by slaying Laius and "polluting his bed," will he be able to avoid fulfilling that dreaded curse of slaying his father Polybus and being joined in wedlock to his mother Meropè? (He does not yet realize that the curse has already been fulfilled.) In consternation, he exclaims: "Then would not he speak aright of Oedipus, who judged these things sent by some power above man?"

What is this "power above man"? He certainly does not mean the gods, for he prays:

* Oedipus does not even suspect yet that he is Laius' son. The kinship he is referring to is the one which has resulted from the marriage with the late king's widow.

Forbid, forbid, ye pure and awful gods, that I should see that day! No, may I be swept from among men, ere I behold myself visited with the brand of such a doom!

That cruel "power above man," which brands him with such a doom, which marks him as a condemned man, is the curse which has doomed Laius and his house. Later, when the Corinthian messenger reveals the cursed king's identity and when the herdsman confirms the dreadful news, Oedipus at last recognizes what that cruel "power above man" really is:

Oh, oh! All brought to pass — all true! Thou light, may I now look my last on thee — I who have been found accursed in birth, accursed in wedlock, accursed in the shedding of blood!

Thereupon, he rushes into the palace and blinds himself.

This analysis of the play leads to the conclusion that Oedipus' search for his identity was a search for his guilt, a search demanded by his conscience and accompanied by fear; it was an act of contrition. Oedipus did wish to know his guilt and to suffer its consequences. If he had preferred to save himself from exposing his stigma, from suffering and shame, he was free to do so. However, his realization of heaven's hatred, his fear of the gods, and in particular his conscience, forced him into the keenest awareness of his impurity and that of his city. "For even if the matter had not been urged on us by a god," he reproached the Thebans, who had neglected to avenge the murder of their king Laius, "it was not meet that ye should leave the guilt thus unpurged . . ." Though broken by self-pity, blameless on account of the innocence of his intentions, he accepted his obligation to atone and to sacrifice his power and the love and esteem of his people. His atonement was furthermore confirmed by his self-inflicted punishment, by his self-mutilation and by his choice to live on as an outcast, as a blind and helpless beggar. He, like Jocasta, could have chosen death, had he not been driven by another force than his mingled shame, fear, and despair. Indeed, the Chorus wonders about the reasons behind Oedipus' strange insistence on suffering: "Thou wert better dead than living and blind." Suicide, however, would have denied the demand of his conscience for atonement, and this demand found confirmation in his choice of suffering: ". . . I have sinned such sins as strangling could not punish."

It must be emphasized that Oedipus did feel guilty, not only of his evil deeds, committed without awareness of their sinful nature, but also of the inherited and as yet unpurged sins of Laius; and thus he felt guilty of not having done his duty to the gods: ". . . all should thrust away the impious one, — even him whom the gods have shown to be unholy — and of the race of Laïus!" His self-mutilation, his blinding, is part of his purging; it is an act of self-punishment and one of the means of atonement. But this, admittedly, does not explain the act entirely.

It was Jung who said that a primitive man thinks in images. When he thinks of his dead mother, he does so by recreating a visual image of her. This means that since his memories are predominantly visual, his mind is identified with his eyes and if he desires to free his mind of an obsessing thought, he really has to extirpate the image and thus also his eyes. However terrible and puzzling the act of self-blinding may appear to us, it is not likely to have meaning beyond conveying utter despair and even madness caused by some crushing frustration. But if, with Jung, we assign to the visual image the same function as we do to thought, the act of blinding oneself assumes far greater significance. Obviously, to commit such an act, one needs the impetus created by powerfully stirred emotions, but these by themselves do not explain this particular kind of self-mutilation and a particular meaning has to be ascribed to it.

To the same degree that we value our power of abstraction and generalization as our most important means of fathoming the interrelationships of life, others, to whom concrete phenomena are valuable because of their immediate significance, may ascribe importance to their visual perception. Just as we may consider the loss of the one faculty as the most crushing blow, so others may consider that the loss of one's eyesight exceeds the loss of all man's other treasured possessions, and the suffering caused by it may drown out any other excruciating pain.

22

Let us now consider Oedipus' act and the expressed and implied reasons for it. The messenger, who precedes Oedipus on the stage, reports on the dreadful happenings in the palace. He quotes the words which Oedipus uttered as he was blinding himself:

No more shall ye behold such horrors as I was suffering and working! long enough have ye looked on those whom ye ought never to have seen, failed in knowledge of those whom I yearned to know — henceforth ye shall be dark!

He is punishing his eyes for failing in knowledge, he is punishing his eyes for having glanced at sin, and by blinding himself he is shutting out from his mind the image of the horrors he has endured and of the horrors he has caused.

It has to be borne in mind that the whole play takes place against the background of the plague and this catastrophe, too, is the result of Oedipus' guilt. His appearance before the Thebans through his desire "to show to all Cadmeans his father's slayer . . . as purposing to cast himself out of the land, and abide no more, to make the house accursed under his own curse . . ." is also an act which forms part of his atonement. He appears in order to prove his desire to purge the house of Cadmus and the city of Thebes, and to do his duty toward his fellow men. But his appearance before the Thebans has added significance if we assume that his blinding was also an act by which he wished to demonstrate visibly his physical suffering and piteous weakness, and thus to prove that his pain equalled the pain he had caused:

MESSENGER

. . . Howbeit he lacks strength, and one to guide his steps; for the anguish is more than man may bear. And he will show this to thee also . . . and soon thou shalt behold a sight which even he who abhors it must pity.

His blinding, then, is also the proof he brings of his compassion, of his sorrow. This is his way of asking for forgiveness by begging for pity.

We shall later witness a similar scene in Samain's *Polyphème*, though there the motives and purposes are different. With Oedipus this is an act of expiation, a truly sacrificial act, as is his desired self-banishment, whereby he intends to atone for his sins against the gods and for his sins against men. And, having performed this sacrifice with his own hands, having brought his broken heart as an offering to the gods, he who has been "found evil, and of evil birth," he, the king, must now offer himself to his people. They, too, have been suffering because of their guilt at having failed to avenge the death of Laius, and Oedipus tells them:

. . . haste ye, for the gods' love, hide me somewhere beyond the land, or slay me, or cast me into the sea, where ye shall never behold me more!

This is not the sacrifice of a man who does not cherish life. Indeed, his self-sacrifice, based on his devotion to the gods and to his fellow men, is sublime because of his keen realization that he is giving up, out of a sense of duty to the one eternal life, that which he holds most dear in his ephemeral existence. This is the very essence of this tragedy. The constantly recurring theme of self-pity is based not only on Oedipus' discovery of having been found evil, but also on his having to give up the pleasures resulting from his love for what is transitory: the pleasure of seeing, the power of enjoyment, the lure and the great satisfaction of crown and power. The desire to eliminate from his experience the sight of what may cause him spiritual pain, and thus to shut out one source of his self-pity — "for it is sweet that our thought should dwell beyond the sphere of griefs" — is also a motive in that complex act of self-blinding. Tears and lamentation, far from reducing the stature of Oedipus, actually measure his devotion to his cause, to his belief, and to his values. They provide the measure of the pain and sorrow which are part of his heroism.

Antigone

CREON, in the *Antigone* of Sophocles, seems to offer a rather striking example of the theory of tragedy as we have seen it formulated in S. H. Butcher's *Aristotle's Theory of Poetry and Fine Arts.* Creon is truly engaged in an unequal struggle with destiny; through his ruin the disturbed order of the world is restored and the moral forces reassert their sway.

Creon's tragic flaw is his rashness and stubbornness. He is proven to be wrong in trying to impose his own order — to him fully justified — against the established divine order, and his stubbornness is broken with the realization of his sinful presumption. Yet it appears that Creon merely experiences defeat, but there is no realization; this crushing experience does not actually lead him to change his view of life according to which, in matters of state policy, the human order takes precedence over the divine order — indeed, according to which the divine order is only recognized insofar as it protects the state.

This is what Weinstock suggests in his earlier mentioned *Sophokles.* According to him,* Creon is the victim of the *Tragik des Zuspät*, of the tragic of the too-late. Instead of rushing to Antigone's rescue, he performs, without conviction, the burial of Polynices, and when he reaches Antigone, it is too late. His sudden religious concern becomes the cause of his ruin.

This analysis shows Creon's stubbornness and single-mindedness

* See his chapter on *Antigone*, pp. 130–162, for fuller discussion.

in a broader perspective than its explanation as a mere character trait would do. His view of life, says Weinstock, determines Creon's single-mindedness and causes the tragic of the too-late to bring about his ruin. For it is not Creon's insight into and acceptance of the law, in the name of which the blind seer Tiresias calls upon him to bury Polynices and thus respect the will of the gods, that prompts him to yield; it is no change of heart, no willingness to live and act according to values recognized as superior, but merely the fear of retribution that drives him to appease the gods by burying Polynices instead of first liberating Antigone from her prison. To Creon, then, Antigone is still guilty of disobedience and therefore does not require first consideration. Granted, Creon is "rash," but his rashness is due to his continued adherence to the paramount claims of the state and throne, which his view of life fully justifies.

Other passages in the play seem also to support Weinstock's interpretation and reveal, in this light, their deep meaning. Faced with the contempt and hatred of his son Haemon, faced later with the complete extinction of his family, Creon feels his guilt but does not seem to understand it:

Ah me, this guilt can never be fixed on any other of mortal kind, for my acquittal! I, even I, was the slayer, wretched that I am — I own the truth.

He bemoans his fate, his "sins of a darkened soul, stubborn sins," and "the wretched blindness of my counsels." Yet, it would be vain to search for any expression of compassion for Antigone. Creon has the self-pity of Oedipus and Antigone, but not their compassion for others, nor, indeed, their courage of renunciation and self-denial for the sake of a superior value:

Ah me, I have learned the bitter lesson! But then, methinks, oh then, some god smote me from above with crushing weight, and hurled me into ways of cruelty, woe is me, — overthrowing and trampling on my joy!

It seems clear enough that Creon is not even willing to accept responsibility for his cruelty, in spite of his previous eloquent justifications of his attitude. He did learn a bitter lesson when

26

he lost his son and wife and he had no other choice but to link these misfortunes to his decree that had sent Antigone to her death. It was obvious to him that he was being punished for having defied the divine law, but it was only through the weight of the punishment that he recognized the seriousness of his error. In the punishment he recognized his sin and broke down, whereas Oedipus recognized his punishment in his sin and atoned. Oedipus asked for his death to spare his city; Creon asked for his as a punishment for having failed in his attempt at "the ordering of the future." To Creon, his view of life, his rigid order, bereft of divine protection, are proven to be wrong, but wrong only because of their consequences, not wrong in and by themselves. Creon has learned to pray and to admit that "the ordering of the future rests where it should rest." But he is, as Weinstock pointed out, merely frightened into submission without showing any evidence of a change of heart.

If the tragic is defined merely in terms of an inevitable doom which follows upon a philosophically and psychologically determined deed or omission, it is justifiable to accept the tragic of the too-late as a determining characteristic of a tragic action. The inevitability of deed or omission and doom may not be, however, the only distinguishing mark of the tragic, though it is a necessary one; a distressing but resolutely accepted renunciation for the sake of superior values may also be of the very essence of tragedy. And the tragedies of Oedipus and Antigone are of this latter kind. Indeed, the preceding discussion of the tragic, as it may apply to Creon, was mainly undertaken to point out the difference between the tragedy of endurance and the tragedy of self-denial and renunciation.

While the inherited guilt is inherent in *Oedipus the King*, in which the tragic issue is brought about by the realization of its import and by sacrificial acts prompted by self-denial, its role in *Antigone* is rather peripheral and in no way affects the course of the dramatic action. Here the action is fully determined by Antigone's free choice and resolution.

Her brother Polynices, killed in his fight against his own

Thebes, after having been dispossessed by his brother Eteocles of his share of the crown, lies unburied and "none shall grace him with sepulture or lament, but leave him unburied, a corpse for birds and dogs to eat, a ghastly sight of shame." This is Creon's order and "whoso disobeys in aught, his doom is death by stoning before all the folk."

Not until we realize the meaning of this edict, shall we comprehend Antigone's determination to defy Creon. Not until we appreciate Antigone's determination in the light of her view of life, shall we comprehend her character. To understand the meaning of the edict from Antigone's point of view, — it is the meaning the edict has for her that determines the direction of her action — it is necessary to appreciate the significance of an "honoured burial" and "unburied shame."

To refuse burial meant to the Greeks to inflict the worst disgrace on the dead, to refuse him "honour among the dead below." To bury Polynices is to Antigone an act of duty imposed by family ties, and her disregard of this sacred duty would be an act of treason: "False to him will I never be found." But above all, she, like her father, is mindful of her obligations to the beyond and of her obligation to preserve her innocence and purity in the eternal life:

I will bury him: well for me to die in doing that, I shall rest, a loved one with him whom I have loved, sinless in my crime; for I owe a longer allegiance to the dead than to the living: in that world I shall abide forever.

She also emphasizes to her sister, Ismene, her devotion to the gods and her will to honor their laws: ". . . if thou wilt, be guilty of dishonouring laws which the gods have established in honour." Similarly, defying Creon's power, she shows herself duty-bound to the gods, and thus to eternity:

. . . for it was not Zeus that had published me that edict; not such are the laws set among men by the Justice who dwells with the gods below; nor deemed I that thy decrees were of such force, that a mortal could override the unwritten and unfailing statutes of heaven. For their life is not of to-day or yesterday, but from all time, and no man knows when they were first put forth. Not through dread of any human pride could I answer to the gods for breaking *these* . . .

It is this concern for the beyond, for her duty to the gods and to her kin which forms the content of her nobility and it is, no doubt, with this in mind that she tells Ismene: ". . . thou wilt soon show whether thou art nobly bred, or the base daughter of a noble line."

In contrast with this belief, with these paramount values, are Ismene's fear of suffering, her attachment to her earthly life, and her obedience to transitory power and law:

And now *we* in turn — we two left all alone — think how we shall perish, more miserably than all the rest, if, in defiance of the law, we brave a king's decree or his powers.

Ismene's weakness and fear, born of her attachment to life, shed light on Antigone's courage and strength which are inspired by her vision of eternity. "One world," says Antigone to Ismene, "approved thy wisdom: another, mine." These visions determine the sisters' attitudes, which in turn determine their actions: the worldly-wise compromise of Ismene and the inspired fulfillment of Antigone.

One would be mistaken in assuming that Antigone is recklessly throwing her life away, that her eagerness to die is a symptom of foolhardiness. Yet, her cold, proud, and defiant indifference in the face of violent threats seems to bear out such an assumption:

Die I must — I knew that well (how should I not?) — even without thy edicts. But if I am to die before my time, I count that a gain: for when any one lives, as I do, compassed about with evils, can such an one find aught but gain in death?

So for me to meet this doom is trifling grief; but if I had suffered my mother's son to lie in death an unburied corpse, that would have grieved me; for this I am not grieved.

It seems, then, that Antigone would have nothing to lose by sacrificing her life that is so "compassed about with evils." Death seems a welcome escape from her life's wretchedness. But these words assume a different meaning when we realize that Antigone is speaking not only to Creon, the king, but also to Creon, the father of her beloved Haemon, to whom she is betrothed. She knows that this love for Haemon is her weakness, her single attachment to earthly life, and that Creon would want her to "bend before troubles." She knows that her stand must not belie her deed, that she must not waver in facing the fatal consequences of a resolution conceived in piety and dutifully fulfilled. To yield would mean to betray her belief.

This is the reason for her defiance; this is her way of proving to Creon that she does not cherish a happiness the price of which is disloyalty. This fear of her weakness explains her haste and her provocative stand, which are intended to strengthen her self-assurance while she is faced by Creon:

Why then dost thou delay? In thy discourse there is nought that pleases me — never may there be! — and so my words must needs be unpleasing to thee. And yet, for glory — whence could I have won a nobler, than by giving burial to mine own brother? All here would own that they thought it well, were not their lips sealed by fear.

Only once does she permit herself to mention Haemon; when Creon suggests that his son has chosen an "evil wife," she cries: "Haemon, beloved! How thy father wrongs thee!" It is in Haemon's defense, not in her own, that she reveals her feelings.

It is not so much the fearlessness with which she braves the might of the king in defense of her convictions that makes Antigone heroic; it is rather her desperate self-denial, with which she overcomes her fear of death and her desire to live, that lends her that heroic stature. Only when her fate has been irrevocably determined, when Creon has left and there is no longer any need for her to fear that her desire to live and love might cause her to weaken and bend, only then does she reveal her pain and her sorrow:

See me, citizens of my fatherland, setting forth on my last way, looking my last on the sunlight that is for me no more; no, Hades who gives sleep to all leads me living to Acheron's shore; who have had no portion in the chant that brings the bride, nor hath any song been mine for the crowning of bridals; whom the lord of the Dark Lake shall wed.

Antigone bewails repeatedly the fate which forces her to sacrifice her earthly life and die "most miserably of all, before the term of [her] life is spent." She realizes the price she is paying for her steadfastness and her convictions:

Such was the law whereby I held thee first in honour; but Creon deemed me guilty of error therein, and of outrage, ah brother mine! And now he leads me thus, a captive in his hands; no bridal bed, no bridal song hath been mine, no joy of marriage, no portion in the nurture of children; but thus, forlorn of friends, unhappy one, I go living to the vaults of death.

Not even Haemon's love can bring her consolation; for she is under guard and is not aware of his courageous effort to save her life.

She knows of no sin of her own, and her act of piety has caused none to suffer but herself. She hopes to be found innocent and virtuous in the eyes of the gods, but she feels that her very innocence and virtue make her guilty and reprehensible in the eyes of men. This leads her to suspect some guilt to be attached to her own life though she knows herself to be innocent and her suffering to be the inevitable consequence of her devotion to the gods and of human injustice:

O city of my fathers in the land of Thebè! O ye gods, eldest of our race! — they lead me hence — now, now — they tarry not! Behold me, princes of Thebes, the last daughter of the house of your kings, — see what I suffer, and from whom, because I feared to cast away the fear of Heaven!

This is sacrificial martyrdom, tragic martyrdom. It has grown out of self-denial and renunciation, and the suffering has been borne heroically, that a divine law might prevail.

It should be noted that Antigone's suicide in no way detracts from this conception of her attitude and fate, since suicide was not regarded by the Greeks as sinful. Oedipus, contrary to the Thebans' advice, did not choose suicide to punish himself, for he believed his sins to be so great as to demand an even harsher means of atonement. By no means did suicide signify a cowardly escape, since life was believed to be eternal. Antigone merely fulfilled Creon's decree and thereby, acting as a tool of the gods, she precipitated Creon's own doom.

The heroism of Oedipus and Antigone is based on their faith, on their belief in paramount values, and on their determination to make their convictions prevail without compromise. Through their suffering they achieve the fulfillment of their recognized human obligations toward deity. This is what lends them heroic stature. Their subordination to duty of happiness, joy, and pleasures — a subordination at the price of keen suffering — lends them tragic stature. It is important to realize that for each of them, the acceptance of martyrdom and self-sacrifice is an act of self-denial and renunciation. They do not have what is known as the passion of martyrdom; they do not rush to their death, nor do they try to secure heavenly bliss by suffering. They sacrifice themselves to re-establish the validity of an order which they themselves or others have violated.

It must also be remembered that they could have acted otherwise. Oedipus, cleared by the people of Thebes of any suspicion and reassured by Jocasta, could have relinquished the search for the culprit when his suspicions pointed to his own guilt. He could have saved his crown, his power, and even his earthly happiness by consoling himself with the fact that he was personally innocent. Antigone could have chosen to follow her sister's advice; she could have avoided becoming involved in a struggle to which her strength was not equal. She could have consoled herself with being a mere woman who was not required to undo the harm caused by evil or to challenge the power of her king. She could have waited, like Electra, for an Orestes to avenge the wronged, for she was going to marry Haemon, the king's son. She could have saved her life, which was showing promise of happiness. Both Oedipus and Antigone acted as their concept of duty and of right and wrong dictated. Yet this knowledge of duty, of right and wrong, would not, alone, provide the strength for self-sacrifice.

32

What is the driving force behind their actions? It is not fear, as in the case of Creon; it is rather their faith in a divine order, and thus their conscience, which gives them the strength for renunciation and for the dutiful fulfillment of what appears to them man's moral destiny. Theirs are not sacrifices made for the glory of some deity, or for self-glorification, even though the feeling of accomplishing a glorious deed may not be lacking in Antigone. These are sacrifices made for the sake of a divine order, for a law. Here homage is paid to the sanctity of the divine law, and testimony is given of an abiding faith in the forces that guard the one way of life by which man is raised to the level of dignity that makes him worthy of entering the eternal and divine stream of life. The self-sacrifice in *Oedipus the King* and the martyrdom in *Antigone* are, then, acts resulting from a sense of duty and, at the same time, acts of renunciation.

The relationship between self-sacrifice and renunciation is important, for in it lies the tragic significance of a self-sacrificial act. To do what one believes to be one's duty is a virtuous act; to do it in the face of danger is heroic; the act is tragic if the virtuous and heroic act leads to an unavoidable doom which is clearly envisaged by the hero who renounces the bliss of earthly life, who tears himself away from the lure of living for no other reason than to fulfill his duty. Complete renunciation and complete fulfillment of duty are the essential elements of the tragic in these plays.

Polyeucte

IT IS important to consider the motivations of the act of renunciation, and of the fulfillment of duty. Instead of being an act of pure devotion, renunciation could be an act of despair, or the result of a conscious or unconscious feeling of insufficiency as in the case of the proverbial sour grapes. In such instances, renunciation is imposed and not freely chosen. Likewise, the fulfillment of duty could be imposed by vanity, by the desire to retain the esteem of others, or even by self-esteem, the pride of achievements which preserves a man's self-respect as he identifies the views he holds of himself with others' evaluations of his worth.

It is possible for a man to do his duty without fulfilling the dictates of his conscience; he may do the right thing for the wrong reason, or at least not for the right thing itself, but for ulterior reasons. He may then renounce, or do his duty, because of an inability to choose to act differently. He may do so, as is well known, without admitting to others, or even to himself, that ulterior reasons are forcing upon him acts which seem virtuous, heroic, or tragic; and he may actually experience them as such because of his instinctive unwillingness and inability to see their full meaning. He may sacrifice himself and fulfill the dictates of duty, in order to prove to others and to himself his worthiness and strength. This general consideration of the possible motives for renunciation is important for an understanding of the complexity of motivations in Corneille's *Polyeucte*.

34

It is also helpful, in approaching the study of this play, to point out what new, extraneous material was added to the source material by the author. Corneille himself provides this source material, a story taken from Surius, a sixteenth century German monk. The following is a brief summary of Corneille's description of the story as he found it. Polyeucte and Nearchus, both Armenian noblemen, are devoted friends. Nearchus is a Christian, whereas Polyeucte is still a pagan, though strongly inclined to become a Christian. In Nearchus' opinion an edict of the emperor Decius, directed against the Christians, threatens their friendship. He fears that it could not last in view of the suffering to which Christians would be exposed and in view of the people's enmity, which would separate them from the rest of the population. Polyeucte is able to reassure his friend: "You do not have to fear at all," he says to him, "that the emperor's edict should disunite us. Last night I saw Christ whom you adore." In this dream Polyeucte saw Christ dressing him in shining clothes, discarding his soiled ones, making him mount on a winged horse and bidding him to follow his lead. It is this vision that has made him decide to do what he had long been intending to do: to declare his convictions publicly and to be baptized.

Polyeucte has been used to listening with respect and admiration to Nearchus' readings about Christ's life and teachings. Filled with enthusiasm he would exclaim: "Oh, Nearchus, if I did not believe myself unworthy to go to Him without having been initiated into His mysteries and without having received the grace of His sacraments, you could see me die eagerly for His glory and in the defense of His eternal truths!" As soon as Nearchus has assured him that it is possible to deserve paradise even without baptism, Polyeucte, seized by pious enthusiasm, spits on the emperor's edict, tears it to pieces, and scatters it to the wind. He tears away the idols from the worshipers and tramples them under foot, thereby astonishing everybody, and Nearchus in particular, with this surprising zeal.

Felix, the emperor's governor of Armenia and Polyeucte's father-in-law, was to enforce the persecution of the Christians in his province. He is grieved to see that Polyeucte's action, besides creating domestic problems, will lose for his provincial government the important support of Polyeucte's highly influential family. He tries to shake Polyeucte's determination to remain a Christian, at first by kindness, then by threats, and even by having him beaten. Finally he sends Pauline, his daughter, to move Polyeucte with her tears. Not only does Felix not succeed in changing Polyeucte's mind, but Polyeucte's heroic example actually causes many pagans to turn Christian. Desperate, Felix orders his son-in-law's death, and Polyeucte goes to his martyrdom "without any other baptism than the baptism by blood," in order to "take possession of the glory God had promised to those who would renounce themselves for the love of Him." That is what Corneille found in Surius about the incident.

The character of Polyeucte that emerges from this account is quite convincing: a fairly young man, impetuous, possessed with an idea, willing to fight and to die for it, willing to sacrifice his position and his family in the defense of what he considers to be right. He is a hero, fired with the zeal of a powerful conviction, a hero Corneille would choose for his courage and determination, for his vision of a supreme value, for his passionate and imperturbable stand, and for a magnificent display of will power. Polyeucte's eagerness to give up his life and to disregard his wife and family point to a state of mind in which his conviction, for whose sake every other value is renounced, appears paramount; but at the same time, and perhaps primarily, Polyeucte intends his sacrifice to be regarded as a convincing testimony to his devotion, as a proof of the purity of his intention to serve his chosen cause willingly and joyfully. The pain of self-denial, the distress over the suffering caused, in the name of a superior value, to those one loves, turn here into self-righteous joy, into a feeling of triumph.

This is the character, the martyr, whom S. H. Butcher, as has already been pointed out in the introductory chapter, excludes from the realm of the tragic because his death represents "moral triumph":

The death of the martyr — of the hero who leads a forlorn hope — of the benefactor of mankind who bears suffering with unflinching fortitude, and through suffering achieves moral victory — fills us with emotions of wonder and admiration; but it can hardly produce the thrill of fear or tragic awe, which Aristotle rightly felt to be an indispensable factor in true tragedy.

We have already seen, however, that besides the experience of physical suffering and pain which the martyr bears "with unflinching fortitude" and through which he "achieves moral victory," he may also experience the suffering and distress which are caused by renunciation. We have seen that renunciation may be a tragic experience which can produce "the thrill of fear or tragic awe" if the martyr's will to live suffers defeat, if happiness and a cherished life are given up in a distressing conflict between worldly and spiritual aspirations. It is only that sense of suffering brought about by persecution or death that is lost in the martyr's moral triumph; the sense of suffering caused by *renunciation*, by the defeat of the martyr's will to live, is not overshadowed by the sense of moral triumph.

There is no doubt that Corneille intended to portray in Polyeucte a hero who adheres to higher values after his baptism than before it. Before his baptism, the greatest good he knows is his love for his wife, Pauline, whom he loves more than his life; but after it, the greatest good he knows is God. This knowledge is supposed to change his values; though still placing his love for Pauline above his life, he does recognize God as the supreme good to which everything else must be subordinated. But Corneille's additions to the plot, which he called "inventions and theatrical embellishments," produced a shift in emphasis from the religious to the worldly that he may neither have intended nor desired.

His play begins with a scene in which Polyeucte shows his loving concern for his wife Pauline. They have been married for only two weeks and Pauline, having dreamed of her husband's death, tells him about the dream and implores him not to leave the palace on that day. Yet that is the day on which Polyeucte has secretly planned to be baptized. To please his anxious wife, he tries to postpone his baptism. Nearchus, who was to have accompanied him, is surprised to see his fearless warrior friend alarmed because of dangers foreshadowed by a mere dream. Nearchus' mistaken assumption permits Polyeucte to show his tender feelings:

> Thou knowest not what it means to have a wife.
> Thou knowest not her hold upon one's heart
> When, after she hath long enchanted us,
> The marriage torches have at last been lit.
>
> . . . .
>
>   I disdain
> Her terrors; I have yielded to her tears.
> She rouses pity in me, but no fears;
> And, touched though unafraid, my heart can nowise
> Make her to whom it doth belong unhappy.
> Is there, Nearchus, so great need for haste
> That I must pay a loved one's sighs no heed?

Polyeucte is not willing to hurt the woman he loves. He is touched by her love, he is happy to be loved and he "does not dare to displease" her. The baptism can wait and must not take place at the risk of causing suffering or even displeasure.

Many critics * have attributed undue prominence to divine grace in this play. Corneille's important contribution to the story is seen in his placing the baptism at the beginning of the play. This, it is claimed, not only allows divine grace to become the most important character in the play, but also explains the miraculous events that follow the baptism. This arrangement of the plot differs from that of the original source, in which the actual baptism never takes place. If we assume that divine grace determines the goals of Polyeucte, even if not the manner in which he tries to reach them, the meaning of the events fills us with emotions of wonder and admiration, to use Butcher's phrase, and the play, however inspired and inspiring, is deprived of its tragic content. On the other hand, the actual text of the play,

* Especially Professor J. Calvet in his *Polyeucte de Corneille* (Paris: Editions Mellottée, 1944).

Corneille's introduction of Severus into the plot – which made
it possible for him to develop his Cartesian theory of love – and
Polyeucte's need to live up to Pauline's concept of merit on which
her love depends, justify an interpretation that does allow the
tragic content to emerge.

Polyeucte's Christian friend, Nearchus, realizing Pauline's influence on her husband, suggests that it is divine grace which
has prompted Polyeucte to *seek* baptism and thereby places the
efficacy of grace on Polyeucte's actions prior to baptism:

> But canst thou know with certainty that thou
> Wilt live till then or feel the same as now?
> Hath God, who holdeth in his hand thy soul,
> Thy life-days, promised thee as high a mood
> Tomorrow? He is ever just and good,
> But not always with the same efficacy
> His grace descends on us. When we have waited
> Too long with our delays, its beams no more
> Transfix the soul; he ceases to dispense them,
> Or else our hearts are hardened 'gainst his grace
> And keep it out. His hand which gave it freely,
> Grows parsimonious, and that blessed zeal
> Whence good proceeds is felt by us but seldom
> Or not at all. The fervor which hath urged thee
> To hasten to baptism wanes already
> And is no more the same; and for the sake
> Of a few sighs which thou hast heard, its flame
> That fired thee flickereth and will soon be dead.

If it is divine grace that animates Polyeucte prior to his baptism
and if, though under the spell of divine grace, he still remains a
considerate, gentle, and loving husband, the baptism itself loses
its role as the source of divine inspiration and of his sudden
change in attitude from gentleness to aggressiveness, from love
to indifference, from simple and sincere devotion to outbursts of
fanaticism.

Thus, this change cannot be ascribed to divine grace; some
other reason needs to be found for the strange and unexpected
display of iconoclasm to which Polyeucte resorts because of an
unexpected but by no means miraculous, turn of events. There

is no need to point, as Professor Calvet does, to the miraculous effects of baptism, known in history, in order to make Polyeucte's actions believable. His actions are quite convincing; the motives underlying them, however, are not necessarily those which affect neophytes, as Professor Calvet expects us to assume, but rather those which the material of the play really suggests.

Polyeucte, the good Christian at heart and the loving husband, feels hurt by Nearchus' distrust:

> Thou knowest me ill. I burn with no less ardor.
> My longing is the more as its fulfilment
> Is further off. Those tears, which I behold
> With a fond husband's eye, leave me at heart
> As much a Christian as thyself thou art.
> But although I prefer above the splendors
> Of empire, as the one supreme good thing
> To which my soul aspires, the consecration
> By that life-giving water which doth cleanse us
> Of sin, makes pure our hearts, unseals our eyes,
> And gives us back man's lost inheritance,
> I think that I can wait one little day
> To soothe a loving wife's anxieties.

Polyeucte seems to rely far more on his own determination and conviction than on grace. He is not postponing his baptism out of fear. A courageous warrior, he feels offended at being accused of weakness and does not wish his love for Pauline to be thus misunderstood. At this point it seems more important to him not to hurt his wife than to hasten to reach "the one supreme good thing" to which his "soul aspires." Yet, later in the play, he will hurt his wife. Are we to believe that "the life-giving water which . . . unseals our eyes" will blind him to his responsibilities, which, before his baptism, he treasures more than, or at least as much as, his spiritual aspirations? One could, indeed, accept baptism as the cause of such a change of attitude if other powerful influences, having the same effect, were not introduced simultaneously.

Nearchus sees in Polyeucte's hesitation and in his concern for Pauline only the work of Satan, the foe of all mankind:

And this dream, filled with black imaginings,
Is but his first device wherewith to stay thee.
He uses prayers and threats and all things else;
Ever he strikes and never doth he tire;
He deems that he can do at last whatever
He cannot do yet, and that anyone
Who will delay is half o'ercome already.
   Frustrate his attack. Let Pauline weep.
God wants no heart which worldly things possess
Or which looks back or, doubtful of its choice,
When *his* voice calls it, hears some other voice.

Polyeucte, shocked, retorts rather provocatively:

Must he who gives himself to God love no one?

And Polyeucte learns from his friend what it means to be a
Christian:

We may love all. He so permits, commands.
But to be frank with thee, this Lord of lords
Doth wish to stand first in our love and honor.
As naught can equal him in majesty,
We must love naught but after him and in him,
Must in his service leave wife, wealth, and rank,
And for his glory pour forth all our blood.
But think how far thou art from that devotion,
Required of thee, which I would have thee feel!
I cannot speak except with tearful eyes.
Polyeucte, we are hated everywhere,
And men believe they do the realm a service
In persecuting us, and any Christian
Is subject to the cruelest tortures. How,
Then, canst thou rise superior to such trials
If thou canst not resist a woman's tears?

Far from feeling subdued, Polyeucte proudly places his love and
his pity high among his values:

Thou dauntest me not. The pity that I feel
Beseems the stoutest heart; 'tis not a weakness.
Beauty moves greatly men like me, Nearchus.
We fear to cause it pain, though death we fear not.

And how will Polyeucte face the persecution to which his baptism will expose him? He knows that a Christian of his time is

supposed to find "happiness and pleasure" in cruel tortures but, being of royal blood, of great influence in the country, and the governor's son-in-law, Polyeucte does not consider such a persecution likely to affect him; but should his rank prove to be no protection, his new faith shall shield him from suffering.

> And if I needs must face the cruelest tortures
> And find my happiness and pleasure in them,
> Thy God, whom still I do not dare call mine,
> Will give me strength in making me a Christian.

When he will "bear the glorious mark" of a Christian, he will also know how to withstand the possible trials of his new existence.

It appears, however, that there is some doubt in his mind about his ability to find happiness and pleasure in tortures. In addition, some of his statements suggest rather clearly a certain lack of enthusiasm for a faith which curtails his freedom to adhere to some of his cherished values in life, and he fears that Nearchus might ascribe this slight hesitation to cowardice. The fear of appearing capable of letting down a friend, the fear of showing weakness where there is mere reluctance, seem more decisive in his yielding to Nearchus' insistence on the baptism than the power of conviction. When Pauline approaches, Nearchus begs Polyeucte to escape:

> Fly from an enemy who knows thy weakness,
> Who strikes thee through it with ease, the very sight
> Of whom o'ercomes thee, and who still doth charm
> Thy heart when doing thee the deadliest harm.

Polyeucte tears himself away from his wife, assuring her, without disclosing his secret intention, that he loves her:

> Far more, heaven be my witness, than myself.
> . . . .
> Thy tears have too much influence on me.
> I feel my heart already prone to yield,
> And only by my flight can I resist thee.

At this point we discover how Corneille's most important "invention" changes the original plot. Pauline, in order to justify the fears which her dream has evoked, tells Stratonice, her friend, that in her dreams she saw Severus, the man with whom she was in love when still in Rome, arrive "crowned with victory." She heard him say:

> Transfer
> To whom thou wilt the love that is my due
> Thou faithless woman; and when this day is over,
> Thou wilt have ample time to mourn the husband
> Whom thou hast chosen to wed instead of me.

The introduction of Severus into the plot is not only a dramatic "embellishment" but a decisive change of the plot and of the action. Severus was a virtuous young Roman whom Pauline had not been allowed to marry because he had no fortune of his own. In his despair Severus joined the army to "win undying fame by a brave death." Indeed, he won a victory in the war against Persia and saved his emperor's life, but he himself was supposed to have perished.

Pauline, a true Corneillean character, considers herself to be "an honorable woman" who "can avow without confusion those spontaneous feelings which reason quells." She knows the price of virtue, she knows that unless virtue is put to the test, it may never be revealed: ". . . none is sure of any heart which has never been assailed." She has always known her duty to her father, the duty of the obedient daughter, and though still in love with Severus, she was ready to accept for a husband any man chosen by her father:

> and I always
> Was ready to accept one, and my mind
> Never approved my heart's insurgency.
> Severus had my love, my thoughts, my longings;
> I did not hide from him how much I loved him;
> We wept together, mourning our ill fortune;
> But I could give him only tears, not hope,
> And though his vows were sweet and dear to me,
> My sense of filial duty was unshaken.

Prior to the opening of the play, Pauline had left Rome with her father, Severus had joined the army and been reported dead, and

Polyeucte had become Felix's choice, the husband of dutiful Pauline:

> And I — when I thus found myself betrothed,
> I gave, as duty bade me, unto him
> Who was to be my husband that affection
> Which my heart's wish had given to the other.

However sincere Pauline's devotion to her husband may have been, however deeply she may have felt her dutiful love for Polyeucte, her virtue, devotion and love do not interest us so much in themselves, but rather for the manner in which they affect her husband.

As the play develops, it becomes apparent that Polyeucte has been aware from the very beginning of the content of Pauline's dream. He has also been aware of Severus' role in her life. But Severus has been reported as dead, Pauline has been dutifully and lovingly loyal to her husband and therefore Polyeucte has not been at all disturbed by the fact that his wife, whom he loves and with whom he has found every happiness, has memories.

The secrecy with which he now undertakes to become a Christian is understandable, for in his wife's dream he has just been killed by "an impious band of Christians" and he knows that her fears do not seem unjustified to her:

> Yet still I dread the Christians' plots and spells.
> I fear they will take vengeance on my husband
> For all their brethren's blood shed by my father.

Polyeucte is not as sincere with his wife as she is with him. He does not disclose his new faith because he knows that he would thereby displease her; yet Pauline has avowed her love for Severus, however painful this may have been to her and to Polyeucte. Her sense of honor demanded this sincerity. The more difficult it was for her to satisfy her sense of honor, the greater she felt her merit to be. For the sake of knowing herself to be virtuous and for the sake of making her virtue known, she was quite willing to reveal her wounded heart together with her indomitable spirit. Her honor demanded the subordination of

44

her passions to duty, it demanded a victory of reasoned will over feelings, and above all complete integrity. However painful Pauline's sincere disclosures may have been to Polyeucte, his wife's pure and uncompromising devotion to duty must have been for him a source of consolation and admiration and Severus' death an assurance of her abiding love.

While Pauline aroused his respect and admiration by being sincere, Polyeucte fears that she would receive his sincere disclosure of his adherence to the Christian faith, to the faith of the victims of her father's persecution, with scorn and blame. This newlywed does not yet enjoy a feeling of complete security; he does not dare to reveal a loyalty she does not share, for fear of displeasing her and appearing unworthy of her love. Anxious to rejoin his friend Nearchus and hoping to escape embarrassment and possibly humiliation and defeat, he hurriedly evades — justifying himself with a "thou shalt know some day" — his wife's bitter reproach:

> Thou hast thy secrets which I may not share.
> Oh, what a proof of love!

While yielding to Nearchus' insistence that he not postpone his baptism, Polyeucte hopes to guard his secret, without forfeiting Pauline's trust and admiration, by assuring her that in his undertaking there is more than honor or life at stake.

While Polyeucte is being baptized the news spreads that Severus is alive. Saved by the king of Persia and returned to the court of his emperor, he enjoys great favors. He has just won another great victory and is about to arrive in Armenia to bring the good news and to render thanks to the gods by a sacrifice. Felix, who fears that Severus' real purpose in coming to Armenia is revenge for the loss of Pauline, and for past humiliations, begs his daughter to save them all by seeing Severus and thus averting the ruin which threatens her father. Pauline, who has never ceased loving Severus, is deeply disturbed at the prospect of such a meeting and afraid that her emotions may betray her, but she agrees to meet with Severus so as not to fail in her duty to her father:

PAULINE

I must obey, since thou commandest this.
But oh, the perils to which thou dost expose me!

FELIX

I know thy purity.

PAULINE

It will prevail,
Indeed. 'Tis not the outcome that I dread.
I shrink from the hard struggle and the turmoil
Of soul which my insurgent feelings make
In me already. But, since I must battle
Now with an enemy whom I love, allow me
A little time, that I may arm my heart
Against itself, and so prepare to see him.

Pauline and Severus meet and their words confirm what Felix
and Pauline had foreseen. She assures him that she loves her husband, but she does not leave any doubt in his mind that it is her
sense of duty to which her passions are made to yield. Severus,
provoked, doubts whether Pauline's love for him was love at all,
and receives an answer with which Pauline not only describes her
feelings, her motives, and her values, but in which she also offers
some insight into her relations with her husband which, considering Pauline's integrity and frankness, could not have remained
undisclosed to Polyeucte and could not have left him unaffected.

SEVERUS

O too much loved, who charmedst my soul too well!
Is it thus, then, that one loves? Or didst thou love me?

PAULINE

Too well I have shown thee that I did, Severus;
And if my heart could quench that love's last fires,
Gods! what cruel anguish I would then escape!
My reason, it is true, controls my feelings,
But whatsoe'er its mastery over them,
It rules them by compulsion, like a tyrant,
And though I give no outward sign thereof,
Within me all is turmoil and rebellion.
Some spell thou hast which draws me to thee still.
Though reason rules me, I can see thy worth.

I see it yet, as when it made me love thee,
So much the stronger in its appeal to me
As it is now girt round with power and glory,
As everywhere it brings thee victory,
As I can better know the greatness of it,
And as it never hath belied my hopes.
But that same sense of duty which withstood thee
In Rome and gave me to a husband here,
Again so well resists thy dear attractions
That though my soul is torn, it is not shaken.
'Tis the same virtue, cruel to our desires,
Which thou didst praise of old, while railing at it.
Lament it still, but praise its resolution,
Which triumphs at once o'er thee and o'er my heart,
And realize that one whose sense of duty
Was not so steadfast or sincere could never
Have merited the love of great Severus.

. . . .

Alas, my rectitude, though still triumphant,
Does not hide well enough my bosom's weakness.
These tears attest it, and the unworthy sighs
Drawn from my breast by poignant memories —
Too cruel results of a beloved presence
'Gainst which my sense of duty ill defends me!
But if thou valuest that rectitude,
Preserve my fame therefor; see me no more.
[Spare me the tears which to my shame I shed,] *
Spare me the feelings which reluctantly
I quell. In one word, spare me these sad meetings
Which but increase thy agony and mine.

This is the state of mind in which Polyeucte finds Pauline after his return. The tears she has shed, he thinks were shed for him. He hastens to console her by proving to her how wrong she was to attribute any credence to the dream which caused her alarm. He knows that Severus has arrived in Melitene, but he does not fear his presence:

I am in Melitene,
And be Severus e'er so great, thy father
Rules here and I am much esteemed by all;

* "Epargnez-moi des pleurs qui coulent à ma honte." This line has been omitted from Lacy Lockert's translation.

> Nor do I think that one can reasonably
> Fear treachery from the heart of such a hero.
> I was told that he was paying thee a call,
> And I was coming to show him the respect
> That he deserves.

Pauline, the virtuous wife who had no secrets from her husband, assures him that once more she has done what her duty bade her to do:

> He has just gone from me,
> Sad and with mind in turmoil; but I have
> Obtained his promise ne'er again to see me.

Polyeucte, apparently unable to understand that this is Pauline's way of reasserting her virtue, interprets her words as expressions of consolation which he feels she may have considered necessary. He has felt Severus' superiority and he has tried to reassure himself as well as Pauline with his own importance in Melitene. Does Pauline now think that he needs reassurance of her continued devotion? Does Severus mean to her again what he used to mean? Has she already detected these fears in her husband? "What! thinkest thou I am already jealous?" he asks with suspicion and in his own defense.

But Pauline believes that she has done everything to allay his, no doubt quite justified, misgivings by her self-denial and her devotion:

> Nay, I would thus insult all three of us.
> I seek mine own peace, which his sight disturbs.
> Even the most steadfast virtue takes no risk.
> To expose oneself to danger courts disaster;
> And, to speak frankly to thee, since true worth
> Can breed love, his continual presence here
> Might well rouse mine. Not only must one blush
> To find one's heart thus taken by surprise;
> One suffers in resisting it, one suffers
> In saving oneself from it, and though virtue
> Can triumph over love, its victory is not
> Easy, the struggle fills one's breast with shame.

Polyeucte is not to be jealous, for that would mean suspecting her virtuousness, which is above suspicion. He is to take her virtue

48

for love, he who has only been married for two weeks. He is to applaud her successful struggle and her escape from the dangers of falling in love again with Severus who is of "true worth." All he can see is that she really loves Severus, that she "suffers in resisting" that love and in "saving herself from it," that she has to make her virtue "triumph over love" for Severus. No doubt, Pauline is sacrificing her love out of a pure sense of duty. Her virtue is not easily victorious. Since she does love Severus, she feels guilty and her "struggle fills her breast with shame."

Polyeucte is not only in love with his wife, but he also admires her strength and courage. Indeed, she makes him feel all too clearly her superiority of character and at the same time the superior worth of Severus. Shall he accept her sacrifice? Shall he show himself less virtuous, less ready for self-denial than the woman who deserves his admiration for these very qualities? Shall he indulge in his happiness, exploit his rights while Pauline appears so deeply moved by the noble sacrifice and the self-restraint of Severus who for love of her and to prove his devotion made his "grief yield" to save her honor? Shall he, Polyeucte, be the only one to live happily at the cost of his wife's suffering and tears, he who loves her "more than himself"? Shall he accept Severus' grief and turmoil; shall he accept a sacrifice from a hero whom he is forced to admire?

> O utter purity! O soul of honor!
> How greatly must Severus feel his loss!
> Thou makest me happy at his heart's expense
> And ever art considerate of my love.
> The more I see my own faults,* and the more
> I think of thee, the more I marvel . . .

Polyeucte cannot accept Pauline's and Severus' generosity and remain indebted to them without hurting his self-esteem. Nor can he refuse their generosity without offending them and especially without hurting his wife, who would be grieved to find her magnanimity wasted on a man who cannot appreciate greatness and is unable to fathom it.

* "Plus je vois mes *défauts* . . ." I believe that *défauts* should in this context be translated by some such word as *insufficiency, inadequacy,* or *imperfection.*

How, then, can he extricate himself from this unendurable situation? He must free himself, but he must avoid losing stature; for such a loss would not only be offensive to him, but to Pauline in particular, since her loving devotion, attached as it is to his moral worth, would be proven misplaced. He must not therefore debase himself in her eyes.

As Polyeucte is about to contrast his own inadequacy with his wife's superiority, he is called by Felix' servant to proceed to the temple, where the assembled people are waiting for him to appear before they offer to the gods their sacrifice in gratitude for Severus' victories. Polyeucte accepts this call without any hesitation and invites his wife to join him. Pauline refuses to go and, unwittingly, sends him to the temple ashamed, hurt, and even humiliated:

> Severus fears the sight of me. It stirs
> His love. I mean to keep my word to him.
> I do not wish to see him any more.
> Farewell, then. Thou wilt see him there. Remember
> His power and the favor he enjoys.

Polyeucte, jealous of his standing, nobly guards his dignity:

> Nay, all his influence does not alarm me;
> And as I know his heart's nobility,
> We shall be rivals in naught but courtesy.

What follows, may by some be regarded as an act inspired by baptism, by divine grace. On this assumption, the action is clear and needs no further elucidation. Here, however, it is proposed to disregard such an interpretation — not, by any means, because such an influence is unlikely, but rather because Polyeucte's action can be understood without reference to the influence of inspiration. Indeed, it actually disproves such an assumption and acquires its true meaning from its human rather than from its supernatural foundations.

Polyeucte is in a dilemma. He loves Pauline and he knows that in her, love is either the result of a sense of duty or of admiration. He also realizes that her love for him is, on the whole, the love of a dutiful wife, while her true love, the "affection which her heart's wish had given," was destined for Severus. To gain that kind of affection, he must arouse her admiration in the same manner as Severus did; and what made Severus worthy was his heroism coupled with magnanimous self-restraint and self-denial. He gave up his great and everlasting love for her to save her "gloire," her honor, her self-esteem, her belief in her own greatness which consisted in overcoming her heart's desires by her virtuous adherence to duty. To equal Severus, Polyeucte must be willing to follow his rival's example. He must not accept her dutiful devotion, he must surpass Severus in magnanimity, he must withdraw. If necessary, he must die — but honorably, for a great cause, for an ideal he can believe in. He must die heroically for a supreme value which can glorify his death. Only by thus surpassing Severus in self-denial and worthy heroism can he win Pauline's true affection.

The dilemma is obvious. In the very act of achieving his purpose, he must defeat it too. In a worthy death alone can he make her see his greatness and win her love. He may conquer her heart, but he must die for his victory; no other honorable withdrawal seems possible. He knows it will be impossible for him to go on living with Pauline without developing a feeling of worthlessness and without losing her devotion for that very reason; he must die, then, heroically and worthily. This form of compensation is a well known pattern of behavior and the motives for it are usually subconscious. The compensatory action is determined by the person's values and beliefs, by the nature of his personal relationships, and by external conditions. Polyeucte, who has just embraced a new faith out of sincere conviction, but without an overwhelming ardor — for the lack of which he was quite severely reproached by his Christian friend Nearchus — now finds in this faith not only a means of satisfying his desire for heroic and sacrificial actions, but also the reassurance that such actions are justified, may even be demanded and, what is more, rewarded by salvation and eternal bliss.

Hardly has he assured his wife that he and Severus, whose "heart's nobility" he knows will not permit him to resort to any other rivalry than that of mutual courtesy, than he suddenly discloses before Nearchus the most unexpectedly aggressive designs. He intends to go to the temple and will not flee the altars as his friend bids him:

> I would fain o'erthrow them,
> Cast them to earth or in their temple die.
> Come, dear Nearchus, let us before all men
> Defy idolatry and show what we are.
> That is the will of heaven; we must obey it.
> I have resolved to do this, and I shall.
> I thank my God, whom thou hast made me know,
> For this occasion, which he so soon hath offered,
> Wherein his grace, ready e'en now to crown me,
> Deigns to make trial of my new-found faith.

Nearchus, who is startled by this behavior, warns Polyeucte: "Too ardent is thy zeal. Do thou restrain it." But Polyeucte cannot restrain it. This is the only way open to him: "One cannot have too much zeal for one's God." This is in sharp contrast with his earlier attempt to delay his baptism, in contrast with his hesitations, his reservations, and his question: "Must he who gives himself to God love no one?"

Nearchus, who knows Polyeucte's love for Pauline and for his life, warns his overzealous friend again: " 'Twill mean thy death." Polyeucte, in a simple and no doubt very sincere answer, reveals the unconscious dichotomy of his motives: "I seek death for his sake." In search of death and glory, he is irresistibly driven to his chosen martyrdom, and Nearchus' insistence that God "hath not bidden us to embrace destruction" meets with Polyeucte's stubborn quest for moral worth:

> The more we do so of our own free will,
> The greater our desert.

Without realizing that Polyeucte has already given up life, Nearchus tries to arouse his friend's will to live:

NEARCHUS
But in this temple thou art sure to die.

POLYEUCTE

A crown e'en now awaits me in the sky.

His simple faith in the prospect of finding reward after death is not only a source of consolation but also a compensation for the "crown" he has lost on earth. In fact, his feeling of having lost all the happiness he hoped to find in life, makes him even more determined to seek and assure for himself the only happiness still left for him, lest he should forfeit this last hope by living unworthily.

Nearchus, steeped in his religion, points out to his barely initiated neophyte that to achieve heavenly bliss "a holy life is needful to deserve it." But Polyeucte's fear of sinful temptations and unworthiness justifies his haste:

> If I live on, my sins could make me lose it.
> Why put in hazard that which death assures?
> Can what will open heaven's gate seem hard?

There is a strange discordance between this revelation of weakness and doubt, and the following reaffirmation of faith which makes it seem as if Polyeucte needs to strengthen his faith before he can find courage enough for the feat he is forced to perform:

> I am a Christian through and through, Nearchus.
> The faith now mine yearns to achieve fruition.
> He who flees hath a coward's faith, a dead faith.

Polyeucte refuses to live, however useful his life may be "to protect the Christians in these regions." He wants his death to be an inspiration for them: "The example of my death will aid them more." But the overriding and avowed purpose of his martyrdom is a worthy and glorious self-sacrifice, for which a crown awaits him in heaven.

Nearchus, still probing and perhaps even doubtful of Polyeucte's motives — he even accuses him of a lack of humility — finally, and without reference to Polyeucte's noble enthusiasm, epitomizes his thinking with this question: "Thou wishest to die, then?" Polyeucte, while unwittingly revealing his changed attitude, startles Nearchus with a concealed reproach: "And dost

thou love life?" Unaware of Severus' role in Pauline's life and
of the nature of her attitude toward Polyeucte, Nearchus is
forced to ascribe his friend's enthusiasm to his baptism. He must
emulate this worthy example with humility:

> Thou comest fresh from baptism, and what fires thee
> Is God's grace, which no crime hath weakened in thee.
> It acts with full force, being still unimpaired,
> And all seems possible to its ardent flame.
> But this same grace, which is in me diminished,
> And which unnumbered sins make ever feebler,
> Acts in great matters so irresolutely
> That naught seems possible to its scant vigor.
> Such spinelessness, such cowardly pretenses
> Are mine in punishment for my offenses;
> But God, whom one should never fail to trust,
> Gives me, to fortify me, thy example.

This explanation of Polyeucte's behavior as inspired by divine
grace is perhaps the basis for some of the one-sided critical ap-
praisals of the play. It must be emphasized that it originates from
Nearchus who was ignorant of Polyeucte's secret motives and
therefore could not see his friend's behavior in any other light.

Pauline, on the other hand, unaware of Poyeucte's adherence
to the Christian faith, can only see the human factors in the
situation. While waiting anxiously for news about her husband's
meeting with Severus in the temple, and still under the fearful
impression of the dream, Pauline ponders in her solitude:

> Severus without cease troubles my thoughts.
> Now I have faith in his nobility,
> And now I fear his jealousy; nor dare I
> Suppose that Polyeucte will without displeasure
> Look on his rival. As hate is natural
> Between these two, their meeting easily
> May terminate in a quarrel. This one will see
> Her whom he thinks should rightly have been his
> Another's wife, that one a desperate man
> Who may attempt some wrong. However high
> The minds that rule their hearts, the one will feel
> Envy, the other anxiety. The shame
> Of an affront that each believes he suffers,

Or has just suffered, or is about to suffer,
Destroys in the first all their patience,
Creates mistrust and anger, and, o'ercoming
At the same time the husband and the lover,
Makes them despite themselves their passions' slaves.
But in what strange imaginings I indulge!
How badly I treat Polyeucte and Severus!
As if these noble-hearted rivals could not
Escape the faults of ordinary men!
They both alike are masters of their souls,
And of too lofty nature for such baseness.
They will behold each other in the temple
Like generous spirits — but alas! they will
Behold each other, and that may be too much!

Stratonice, Pauline's friend, comes to tell her of the sacrilegious acts of Polyeucte and Nearchus: their violence, their "lack of all respect," their scorn and mockery, their blasphemies, and their profanation of the temple. Pauline is shocked to learn that her husband is a Christian and Stratonice freely condemns him:

This heart so great, this nature so divine,
No more is worthy of life, nor of Pauline.
He is no more that husband thou didst love.
He is alike the realm's foe and the gods' foe,
A wicked, infamous, disloyal, faithless
Scoundrel, a traitor, dastard, monstrous villain,
A thing abominate to all good people,
An impious blasphemer — in short, a Christian.

Pauline's attitude in this crisis is the pivot of the action. It is her loyalty as a wife which turns Polyeucte into a tragic character, his acts into tragic acts:

He is all that thou sayest, if he hath
Embraced their faith. But he is still my husband,
And 'tis to me thou speakest.
. . . .
                                        I in duty
Have loved him, and that duty still is mine.

Pauline might have shared her friend's feelings:

He gives thee now good grounds for hating him.

> One who is unto all our gods a traitor
> Could well have been unfaithful unto thee.

If she could have followed this advice, Polyeucte would have ended disdained, scorned, and ridiculed — at least in the eyes of those before whom he wished to appear noble and magnanimous. He would have had to console himself with the thought that his greatness remained misunderstood, or he could even have come to believe in the futility of his self-sacrifice, since his beliefs were not too deeply rooted and since, subconsciously at least, his motives were not serving a single purpose only.

Neither self-admiration nor the feeling of futility is a mark of tragedy. Without sympathetic response Polyeucte would lack tragic stature, though not pathos. The absence of a sympathetic response would, as will be seen in Samain's *Polyphème*, deprive the play of its tragic content. Pauline's steadfastness saves and brings into focus the meaning of Polyeucte's death, the price of his sacrifice, and the sense of the tragic when she tells Stratonice:

> I would have loved him still, though faithless to me,
> And if thou art astonished at such love,
> Know that *my* duty does not in the least
> Depend on him. Let him not do his duty
> If so he pleases; I must yet do mine.

She knows how desperate Polyeucte must have been and how blinded, for "the horrid lengths to which his sacrilegious frenzy went" could find no other explanation. This frenzy, as can be seen, she is ready to ascribe to her husband's jealousy, since she would expect him to act as "a desperate man who may attempt some wrong." She knows that his anxiety and the affront he was about to suffer would destroy all his patience in the first moment of his meeting with Severus, and she expects both rivals to become "despite themselves their passions' slaves." To her, her husband's frenzy seems the expression of his pain, anxiety, and despair, and thus of his wounded dignity. Though it is out of a sense of duty that she still does not "shrink from him," it is significant that she does not condemn his blasphemies because she realizes their hidden meaning. She implores her father to save Polyeucte's life, and her tears, her persistent prayers, and her grief give her love for her husband a new meaning.

Although Pauline "quenched the dearest love e'er worthy of sanction in a gentle breast" to accept her father's preferred choice, she does begin now to feel pity for Polyeucte because of the suffering she has caused him. Pity is now added to dutiful love; an affection bred by pity moves her to implore her father for forgiveness, and in order to save Polyeucte she tries to awaken pity in her father. It seems that subconsciously she is even feeling guilty of having been the cause of Polyeucte's desperate acts. Her duty not to shrink from him is then not only tinged with pity and affection but also with a feeling of obligation to undo the harm she has caused.

There is another important element that enters into the complexity of her feelings and considerations. She knows that Polyeucte is a man of integrity; even though she realizes that jealousy, anxiety, and pain have caused him to act in so crude a manner in the temple, she also knows that, having embraced the Christian faith, he would not hesitate to seek death in the defense of his faith. This is why she tells her father to "give him, outright, his pardon," impressing upon him that her husband is not ready to give in to threats and humiliations:

> If thou still lovest him, give up the hope
> That he will change his faith twice in one day.
> Not only is it that Christians are more steadfast;
> Thou dost expect too great inconstancy
> In him. This is no error thoughtlessly
> Imbibed in childhood with his mother's milk.
> Polyeucte is by deliberate choice a Christian
> And came with firm convictions to the temple.
> Thou shouldst presume he is like all the others.
> Death is to them not terrible nor shameful;
> They glory in their hatred of our gods;
> Blind to the things of earth, they covet heaven,
> And, thinking its gates opened wide by death,
> Care not if they are tortured, maimed, or slain.
> They regard suffering as we do pleasure;

> It leads them to the goal of their desires.
> They call the vilest of deaths "martyrdom."

To Pauline, then, Polyeucte's violence has been the result of despair, but the act itself she justifies on the basis of his convictions.

There is every reason to assume that without Severus' appearance, without the anxiety and pain which it caused, and without the dilemma which resulted from it, Polyeucte would have chosen to become a benevolent protector of the Christians, as Nearchus had hoped and suggested. The secrecy of his baptism does lead to the belief that he had intended, by dignified, considerate, and tactful means, to win the sympathy of his wife and father-in-law for his beliefs and for his cause.

It is also justifiable to maintain that his violence is brought about by the suddenly arisen necessity to seek an honorable and glorious path to self-destruction. Severus chose war for the purpose of seeking an honorable death in the glorious defense of his emperor. Polyeucte chooses a holy war, seeking an honorable death in the glorious defense of his religion. Both are heroic, both would have acted in exactly the same manner as they do, if called upon by duty to defend what they stood for; but neither would have acted in that manner by deliberate choice and without moral compulsion, had he not been driven by despair.

Polyeucte's tragic fate is actually not determined by any fear that Severus might cause him to lose Pauline's dutiful devotion, but rather by his self-imposed refusal to accept her devotion which, while unexposed to any rivalry, he believed to be his wife's deepest expression of love. Since Severus' arrival he has learned to measure its depth, and he cannot yield, however moved he may be by Pauline's tears and however piteously she may entreat him; he cannot accept her love without proving himself first worthier of it than anybody else. He knows now that without attained glory, without signal merit, her devotion cannot turn to love.

To secure this love, he must stand firm and abide by the demands of his faith. By his death alone, then, can he win

Pauline, for to win her love means to win her mind and soul, and this he cannot achieve without magnanimity, without self-denial, and without self-sacrifice. In order to arouse her admiration and turn her dutiful devotion to loving affection, he must live up to her model of valor and heroism and even surpass the worth of his rival by the sublimity of his sacrifice. This is why he has to reject her, deny his marriage, give up his happiness, and destroy himself to free her from the burden of her obligations. He can draw strength from his new faith by believing in the reward of eternal heavenly bliss, and as a martyr he may be able to save Pauline, too; he may save her soul and thus be united with her forever. His martyrdom may alone win for him the crown of worth and the crown of heaven.

Against his belief and his desire for martyrdom, neither of which he can betray without losing his self-esteem and, above all, Pauline, there rises the will to live, which tempts him to give up the yearning for eternity and the passionate desire to win Pauline's soul; there is the temptation to grasp whatever share of happiness he can, however transitory. Pauline's adherence to merit and honor determines his resolution of this conflict, and his attitude is therefore not primary but compensatory. His primary attitude is repressed, but actually not overcome; indeed, the tragic in the play is encompassed by these inseparable and yet conflicting attitudes. The temptations to which he is exposed by Pauline's presence not only fill him with the anguish of a shameful weakness and self-betrayal, but also with the fear of having to suffer the consequences of his weakness — that of seeing his transitory happiness subjected to the fate of all ephemeral phenomena, of necessarily fleeting emotions. The despair and suffering he experiences when he suddenly realizes his past self-deception and sees his illusions shattered, make that fear a very real one.

This state of mind, as he prepares to face Pauline for the first time since he had left her to go to the temple, emerges from Polyeucte's most revealing self-examination, prayers, threats and longings:

The encounter which I dread above all others!
Felix, I triumphed o'er thee in the prison,
Laughed at thy threats, saw thee unflinchingly.
To avenge thyself for thy defeat, thou takest
More potent weapons now. I fear much less
Thy executioners than her distress.
 O Lord, who seest the perils which I face,
Double thine aid in this my urgent need!
And thou who wentest lately hence victorious,
Look on my trials from thine abode of glory,
Nearchus! to o'ercome so strong a foe,
Stretch down a hand unto thy friend below!
. . . .

Source of earth's joys and woes in equal store,
Deceptive pleasures, why trouble me anew?
Shameful bonds of the flesh and the world, wherefore
Do ye not turn from me as I from you?
Begone, delights and honors, my soul's foes! Alas,
Your entire felicity,
Being of the things that die,
Doth in a twinkling change and pass;
And though 'tis bright as clearest glass,
It hath the same fragility.

Hope not that I shall sigh for you again.
To me your powerless charms ye vainly showed —
Yea, showed throughout this empire vast in vain
The rich and prosperous enemies of God.
He shows me in his turn their righteous overthrow:
How these great folk shall be undone,
And how the sword shall fall upon
Their guilty necks and fall but so
Much the surer as its blow
Shall have been foreseen by none.

Tiger athirst for blood, Decius the cruel,
Long hath God left his children in thy power.
See the dread sequel of thy haughty rule:
A little more, and thou shalt reach that hour
When Scythians shall avenge the Persian and
    Christian dead.
Naught can save thee from that doom.
The thunderbolt that is to come,

Cleaving the sky, to cleave thy head
For thy sins, cannot be further stayed
By the hope that thou wilt turn therefrom.

Let Felix sacrifice me to thy wrath.
Let a rival's power blind him. Let him have
My rival for a son-in-law by my death,
And rule here still by making himself a slave.
I care no whit — nay, rather I to my fate aspire.
World, thou no more art aught to me;
My heart, now Christian utterly,
Burns only with a sacred fire;
And as an obstacle to higher
Things, and naught else, Pauline I see.

Delights of heaven, holy imaginings,
How full ye fill the heart that can receive
Such benisons. Those who possess these things,
And know their charm, henceforth cannot believe
That aught could daunt them. Ye promise much; ye
  give yet more.
Your blessings are inconstant never,
And death, to crown my soul's endeavor,
Serves but as a kindly door
To bring us to that blessed shore
Where we shall find content forever.

'Tis thou, O fire divine, which naught can quench,
By whose aid I shall see Pauline, nor blench.
                    (Enter PAULINE.)
I see her, but my heart, which holy zeal
Enflames, no longer now doth feel her spell
As formerly, and mine eyes, that see the light
Of heaven, no more take pleasure in her sight.
  Madam, what purpose makes thee have me brought
    here?
Wouldst thou contend with me or strengthen me?
Is this attempt, which showeth thy love complete,
Meant for mine aid or meant for my defeat?
Comest thou in enmity or in affection,
As my sworn foe or my soul's other half?

Polyeucte knows that his "rival's power" has blinded Felix, and
that Felix would wish to give his daughter to Severus. Polyeucte,

who cares no whit, has hardly any other choice. Even though Pauline and Felix come to save him, he knows for what "deceptive pleasures" as Pauline's husband, for what "shameful bonds" as the emperor's slave, he would be saved. "Let Felix sacrifice me to thy wrath . . ." is not only the disinterested attitude of a man who is about to find salvation in death, it is also the subdued cry of defeat. He needs the consolation of the "delights of heaven," of blessings that "are inconstant never" — he who after two short weeks of marriage and after Severus' reappearance, has learned to value constancy and lasting contentment. These are the "higher things" he has lost, and the only person through whom he might regain them is also the one who has unavoidably caused his loss.

An element of self-deception appears to enter into Polyeucte's zealous faith and makes his ardent belief seem to be the result of despair. It cannot be forgotten, however, that his belief is quite sincere and that it is rather his zeal, his impetuousness, and his ardent desire for consolation and lasting contentment which result from his despair. In vain does Pauline assure him that it is he alone who desires his doom and that he alone can save his life. In vain does she remind him of his noble descent, his "glorious deeds," his "rare abilities," his standing in the country, and his power. Polyeucte has been hurt and disillusioned, and life, however tempting, would necessarily perpetuate his suffering and despair:

> I recall more. These my advantages
> I know, and know what hopes on such foundations
> Ambitious spirits build; yet they aspire,
> If truth be told, only to transient blessings
> Which cares will vex and dangers will attend.
> Death takes these from us; Fortune sports with them —
> Today a throne, a dunghill on the morrow —
> And their bright splendor rouseth so much envy,
> Few of your Caesars have enjoyed them long.
> I have ambition, but 'tis nobler, fairer.
> Those honors perish; I seek immortal honors,
> A bliss assured, eternal, infinite,
> Above the reach of envy and of fate.

Can this flight from envy and fate be the effect of his enlighten-
ment by baptism? It does appear that Polyeucte, in his relation
with God, does not base his devotion on self-denial, on renunciation. Yet, in his relation with Pauline he recognizes the need
for proving his devotion by self-denial and renunciation. Obviously, Polyeucte expects divine protection and heavenly bliss,
and does not remember Nearchus' reminder: "A holy life is
needful to deserve it." Indeed, he seems quite akin to a *libertin*
who, induced by Pascal's proposed wager, would agree to sacrifice his misery in life to gain peace and salvation:

> (A bliss assured, eternal, infinite,
> Above the reach of envy and of fate.)
> Is this too dearly bought with one poor life,
> Which soon and suddenly can be snatched from me, —
> Which gives me joy for but a fleeting moment
> And cannot promise safety after that?

Polyeucte, ironically, does not realize that he is merely consoling
himself in an escape from life which he desperately wishes to
appear to be glorious for the sake of his self-esteem and for the
sake of Pauline, in whose eyes he must outshine Severus:

> I ought to give my lifeblood for my country,
> My sovereign, and his crown; but how much more
> I ought to give it for the God who gave me
> My life! If dying for one's prince be glorious,
> What must it be when for one's God one dies!

It is clear, then, that Polyeucte cannot endure to live; nor can
he bear to return to that reality in which he felt Pauline's hold
over his heart and her enchantment, without having surpassed
Severus and thereby won Pauline's heart. In such a life he would
have to let his passionate love be answered by virtuous kindness
and dutiful affection. He would have to keep reminding himself
of his unworthiness, and accept with embittered gratitude a
thorny happiness which he could not even reject for fear of
appearing more unworthy. He would have to remember that his
mind had been forced to approve, with admiration and applause,

his burning wound inflicted by cold Roman virtue, and he would have to keep repeating:

> O utter purity! O soul of honor!
> How greatly must Severus feel his loss!
> Thou makest me happy at his heart's expense
> And ever art considerate of my love.
> The more I see my own faults, and the more
> I think of thee, the more I marvel . . .

He cannot return to the sadness of this "poor life" and therefore he hastens into the safe harbor of death:

> The mercy of my God is far more precious.
> It saves me from the risks I might have run,
> Leaves me no chance to turn back in my course
> But crowns me ere I have begun the race,
> Wafts me to harbor with the wind's first breath,
> And straight from baptism sends me to my death.
> If thou couldst know how small a thing life is
> And by what ecstasy this death is followed!

Polyeucte sends for Severus, for in his rival's eyes too he must triumph, however costly and painful that triumph may be. He will hand over to his rival his greatest treasure and thereby not only surpass him in generosity, but also free himself of the hold upon his heart which may otherwise lure him into the net of a dreaded life. He will renounce Pauline and ask Severus to accept this gracious gift. If by this act Polyeucte did not intend to rid himself definitely of his fear of succumbing to Pauline's lure and at the same time to surpass his rival's magnanimity before his and Pauline's eyes, he could have allowed developments to take their natural course; he might have trusted that his disregard would hurt his wife sufficiently, so that she would no longer feel any obligation toward a husband who for the sake of a more coveted happiness rejected the one she was able to create for him.

But Polyeucte does not wish to lose her affection; indeed, since he wishes to retain it and make himself worthy of her love, there is left for him no other means to achieve this aim than a heroic and glorious death. Thus he cannot count on reaching his goal while alive and necessarily places his hopes in the beyond. By giving Pauline to Severus and letting her, who "prefers the world to God's forgiveness," live happily, he does not give up his struggle for her soul; indeed, by this generous act he actually hopes to win it:

> I have a treasure which I did not deserve.
> Let me, before I die, give it to thee
> And leave the rarest virtues that were ever
> Bestowed by heaven upon a mortal woman
> To the most honorable and valiant man,
> Adored by all, that Rome hath yet seen. Thou
> Art worthy of her, and she is worthy of thee.
> Do not refuse her from her husband's hand.
> He parted you; his death shall reunite you.
> May a love once so true, never grow less.
> Give her again thy heart; accept her vows;
> Live happily together, and each die
> Like me a Christian. That is the fair future
> That Polyeucte desires for both of you.
> Let me be led to death; I have naught more
> To say. Come, guards. 'Tis done.

Just as Polyeucte felt humiliated by Severus' generosity and Pauline's virtuous self-restraint, so they cannot accept Polyeucte's sacrifice or base their happiness on it. In fact, it almost seems as if Polyeucte had foreseen that and used his offer merely to establish his superiority in self-denial and sacrifice, in honor and glory.

Severus does not leave this challenge unanswered and, though aware that he will gravely displease his emperor, he intends to save this Christian:

> The glory of proving to this noble being
> That I am like her and am worthy of her, —
> That mine she should have been, and heaven's decree
> Wronged me when it denied her unto me.
>
> . . . .
>
> Honor constrains me now, and I will heed it.
> Henceforth let Fate be kindly or be adverse,
> As it by nature is inconstant ever,
> If I die nobly, I shall die content.

Polyeucte's motives become even more apparent when Felix tries to save him from his death:

FELIX

Dost thou, indeed, hate life so bitterly,
Unhappy Polyeucte, and do Christian precepts
Command thee to desert thy family?

POLYEUCTE

I hate not life; I love the living of it,
But am not bound to it with slavery's bonds.
Always am I prepared to give it back
Again unto the God from whom I hold it.
Thus reason bids me feel, and Christian precepts,
And thus I show you all how one should live
If ye have hearts with courage to follow me.

FELIX

Follow thee to the abyss where thou wouldst plunge?

POLYEUCTE

Rather to glory, whither I shall mount.

Of what other slavery could Polyeucte be thinking than that which binds him with a feeling of humiliating inferiority, a happiness endured through the pity and magnanimity of others, and a love which can never be fully reciprocated? Reason, as well as Christian precepts, bids him to flee from unendurable suffering to the one haven of glory and fulfilled expectations which is still left open to him.

In disclosing his reason for his sudden change in attitude, Polyeucte does not even conceal his reproach to his wife:

POLYEUCTE
Wed Severus.

PAULINE
Monster!
Kill me at least without insulting me.

POLYEUCTE

Because I love and pity thee, I seek
To solace thee. I see what grief possesses
Thy soul, and well I know another love

66

Is the one remedy for this. Aforetime
Severus by his true worth charmed thy heart,
And hence, if near thee, he should still be able
To charm it. Thou didst love him; he loves thee;
And now his new-won glory . . .

PAULINE

                        What have I
Done to thee, cruel man, to be treated thus
And be reproached — thou scorning my devotion —
For the great love that I o'ercame for thee?

Polyeucte triumphs over Pauline's dutiful devotion by means
of his pity; with pity he can now refuse to accept from her an
affection which she had imposed on her heart; with pity he can
release her from the burden of duty, for what he wants is not
her devotion but her love — a love born of admiration rather
than of duty, one which does not call for his gratitude, which
has not been the result of her heart-rending victory:

I have already said, and say again,
Live with Severus or else die with me.
I do not scorn thy tears nor thy devotion,
But howsoe'er our love pleads in my heart,
Henceforth I know thee not unless thou art
A Christian.

Only thus could he come to believe that his worth has surpassed his rival's and that her devotion has turned into love.
Pauline would have to prove by her death — for Polyeucte does
not propose to live with her even if she should become a Christian — that she has placed his values higher than life, higher than
Severus' glory, and that her husband's readiness for self-sacrifice
has conquered her soul and made her want to share with him
eternal heavenly bliss and suppress her yearning for earthly happiness with Severus.

As the soldiers are about to lead him to his death — and all of
Pauline's and Felix' efforts at saving him from death have failed
because of his unconquerable obstinacy — Pauline exclaims, though
not yet with "unsealed eyes":

                        I will follow thee
Where'er thou goest, and die if thou dost die.

67

But Polyeucte, afraid that she may follow him still out of a sense of duty, warns and pleads: "Follow me not, unless thou turnest from error." Thereupon she witnesses his death and turns Christian. Whether she does so under the emotional strain of seeing her husband die heroically, out of loyalty or a feeling of guilt, or out of honor and for her "gloire"; whether she is inspired by Grace, or acts out of spite and anger over her father's heartless concerns for political expediency — her motive is of little consequence. Polyeucte's act of martyrdom is completed and, dramatically, the play is at its end.

The main factors, which led in this play to a tragic dilemma, must be sought in Corneille's honor-conscious heroism. "Honor," said de Vigny, "is the poetry of duty." Honor demands a passionate and unconditional fulfillment of what is conceived to be one's duty. Honor is, therefore, the mark of moral strength and of worthiness. It implies devotion to an ideal whose unquestionable value is recognized. This dutiful devotion demands self-restraint, self-denial, and even self-sacrifice. To display such devotion is to acquire honor, which alone lends worth to a human being. Furthermore, it is this honor which makes man worthy of love and devotion, and consequently love itself is the reward of merit. Love is the bond which links admiration to worthiness; the greater the honor, and thus the personal worth, the greater the love.

Pauline is devoted to her husband, for that is traditionally her duty as a wife. Her devotion is tested by disturbing inner conflicts, of which honor must decide the issue. She fulfills her duty heroically and she expects, therefore, recognition for her honorable achievement. She would be deeply hurt to find that her virtuous sacrifice is not appreciated.

Polyeucte, a sensitive and impulsive man, suddenly finds that to avoid offending Pauline he must accept her devotion as love. Pauline's love for Severus, recognized by Polyeucte for what it is, hurts his pride and humiliates him. Unable to accept her sacrifice because it is humiliating, Polyeucte is forced to withdraw in the only manner his love, pride, and vanity, and the concept of honor imposed by Pauline, permit; he must choose honorable death. The tragic lies in this inevitability of death, to which a craving for life is opposed.

There are, however, aspects of the tragic in this play which, when contrasted with those in *Oedipus the King* and *Antigone*, reveal that the conception of tragedy here is basically different from that of the two earlier plays. Oedipus chooses suffering and sacrifices himself because he feels that to be his duty to the gods and to men, to the dead and to the living. He discovers himself to be morally indebted and he acquits himself of his debt. His sacrifice is made dutifully, not willingly, for he loves life. He could have avoided his doom had he been able to live with the suspicion of guilt in his conscience. He bows to the moral order according to which he is determined to govern his life. That order was disturbed, and his doom must re-establish it.

Antigone chooses suffering and sacrifices herself because she feels that to be her duty to the gods and to the spirit of her dead brother. She, too, though for no act of her own, discovers herself to be morally indebted, guilty of a possible sinful omission; and she acquits herself of her debt. Her sacrifice, too, is made dutifully and not eagerly, for at long last she is about to taste the joys and happiness of life. She, like Oedipus, could have avoided her doom, if she could have endured living with the feeling of cowardice and unworthiness in her heart. And so she, too, bows to the moral order to which she is determined to subordinate her life. That order was being disturbed and her doom will re-establish it. Both subordinate vital personal interests to what to them is a dictate of conscience. They sacrifice themselves in order to uphold their superior values.

In the case of Polyeucte it is necessary to distinguish between two kinds of motives which prompt his attitudes and actions. Polyeucte, the Christian, and Polyeucte, the husband of Pauline, have to be viewed separately as well as together. Polyeucte, the Christian, chooses suffering in order to bear testimony to his faith in God. He seeks death in order to save his soul from life's sinful temptations. He renounces life, because it appears inferior to the eternal heavenly bliss he foresees as a reward for giving up transitory worldly pleasures. As a result, his renunciation is marked by eagerness and deep satisfaction. He "bears suffering with unflinching fortitude." He "is ranged on the same side as the higher powers" and it seems that Butcher's verdict on martyrdom in tragedy is fully justified, and that in *Polyeucte* the sense of suffering is lost in that of moral triumph.

If one considers only Polyeucte, the Christian, the sense of the tragic is all lost. "Wonder and admiration" remain our only emotions. In such a partial view, there is no moral indebtedness incurred by Polyeucte, he is not called upon to acquit himself of any such indebtedness, there is no paramount moral necessity for him to seek suffering and martyrdom, his conscience would not make his life unbearable if he did not burst into the temple in order to show everybody who he is. Indeed, such an analysis leads to the belief that without Severus' return, Polyeucte himself would not have seen any necessity to storm the pagan temple after his secret baptism. Viewed only as a Christian, Polyeucte is actually not performing a sacrificial act in seeking his death, for he is giving up what he no longer values.

And yet, this is a tragedy which "shows us a mortal will engaged in an unequal struggle with destiny." Polyeucte, the Christian, is also Pauline's husband and the rival of Severus. This Polyeucte also chooses suffering and thereby bears testimony to his power of self-denial. He seeks death, for it is his only means of avoiding humiliation in his marriage and of surpassing Severus in heroism and esteem. He renounces life because his sense of honor could not make him endure it, but he is also afraid that, obeying his passion for Pauline, the desire to go on living may rob him of the strength to sacrifice his life. This fear of yielding, of betraying his honor and self-esteem, of stooping to servility, is one of the main causes of his eagerness to die; but there is an even more decisive factor in his headlong rush toward death, and that is his fear of the consequences of self-betrayal, of his weakness and servility, which would rob him of even the dutiful devotion of his wife and would change her devotion to disdain and contempt. Ironically, Polyeucte's aroused determination to assert himself, to save his dignity and self-esteem by the only means that could assure his moral triumph, has as its fatal consequence his unavoidable death.

What human strength would suffice, in the struggle against his passions and Pauline's pleading — for to yield to either would lead to his moral defeat — to sustain his will to save his honor and win his wife's loving esteem? His nascent devotion to a high moral cause, his conversion to the belief in eternal salvation, lend justification to his self-denial, purpose to his eager desire for death, conviction of worthiness to his self-sacrifice; they replace the fear of weakness by the fear of sin, and the temptation of his passions by a disdain for them bred by the faith in a blissful eternity.

Fate in this tragedy is a rigid concept of honor, which imposes demands of self-denial and sacrifice. Those who sacrifice in order to uphold the concept of honor are of heroic stature. Those, however, for whom the sacrifice is made, find themselves morally indebted. To save their honor, they must acquit themselves of their debt, but they must not thereby offend the sacrificial spirit which has caused their indebtedness. In order to acquit themselves, they must choose to serve an even higher, and therefore more honorable, cause which imposes an even greater sacrifice on them. Also, they must bear with magnanimity the suffering this sacrifice entails, to prove their complete devotion to the cause. For fear of losing their self-esteem and the esteem of others, they refuse to admit to themselves that they sacrifice themselves for the higher cause primarily in order to acquit themselves of their moral indebtedness. They refuse to see that they do not sacrifice their lives for the cause itself, but to win a moral victory which may establish their personal moral ascendancy. This is not hypocrisy, but rather self-deception. It even seems that they are afraid of having to admit to themselves the embarrassing double purpose of their virtuous sacrifice, and therefore they rush, not without despair, toward their liberating death.

This despair, caused by their fear of betraying their values, of appearing in their naked vanity, of exposing their craving for self-assertion, of revealing their dishonoring weakness, is the source of our pity for man aspiring even at the cost of life, to appear to be, to the point of self-deception, what he anxiously feels he is not. There lies the pathos of spiritual striving which is more easily accomplished by dying than by living, which makes it possible for outward strength to conceal inward weakness and for spiritual faith to repress the despair of life.

Aglavaine and Selysette

MAETERLINCK'S *Aglavaine and Selysette* has many traits which permit the drawing of a comparison between this play and *Polyeucte*, in spite of obvious and considerable differences.

In one of the typical, almost legendary, Maeterlinckian castles live Meleander and Selysette. They are happily married, although Meleander has very little in common with his childlike wife. With them live Selysette's invalid grandmother, Meligrane, who spends the days sleeping in her chair, and Selysette's little sister, Yssaline. The peaceful harmony and calm joy of this carefree existence are suddenly disturbed by a letter announcing Aglavaine's arrival. Selysette's brother has died and left Aglavaine a widow. She is to live in their tender midst and forget the suffering caused by her own unhappy marriage.

Aglavaine is a woman of unusual beauty and her mind is continuously striving toward moral perfection, toward purity of thought and action, toward spiritual beauty. "And now," she writes, "I am happy to have suffered; I shall be able to share with you what I have gained in my sadness." She hopes to bring to them the protection which she believes emanates from people who have appeased the wrath of fate. She believes she brings with her a love for both Meleander and Selysette that will guard them against the misfortune and sadness that befall those whose love does not make them kind and considerate. Her suffering has instilled in her a feeling of pity for those who suffer and for the frailty of those who may suffer.

73

Meleander, who has been living in spiritual isolation, since his thoughts were not answered by Selysette's elusive feelings, is anxiously awaiting Aglavaine whom he believes to be "one of those people who can unite the souls at their source." He foresees that he will be understood by Aglavaine, that he will be able to exchange thought for thought, that he will thereby even learn to understand his wife.

But Selysette, who does not reason, whose experiences are felt and whose feelings are, for the most part, only suggested by gestures, perceives in Meleander's attitude a threat. She fears the loss of her husband's affection, and the mental superiority of Aglavaine which she cannot hope to match. In a flash, she recognizes that her husband is going to find in Aglavaine what he was missing in his relationship with her, that he is going to discover a happiness he had not known with her, whose fault had been that of leaving to her love and affection alone the task of keeping their hearts united. It seems to her that Meleander's thirst for spiritual union with an understanding person is the thirst for love, for that kind of love he cherishes. However, she can only summarize her fear and suspicions in a few words: "Love her if you love her. I will go away . . ." Only her tears express fully the thoughts which have led to this outburst. This intended withdrawal, this resignation, is the protest of her injured weakness, is the soothing of the pain caused by her sudden realization that she is inferior to her husband's ideal.

Meleander recognizes the tears of jealousy, is willing to sacrifice the happiness Aglavaine was to bring to him, and hastens to console his wife; Aglavaine shall not stay. He scarcely realizes, however, how his magnanimity, his consideration and his sympathy are apt to hurt Selysette. Is she to accept his sacrifice and be the cause of his unhappiness, she who has just realized how little she really meant to him? Has she not already been humiliated by this realization? Is she to endure the added humiliation of feeling herself to be unworthy in her husband's eyes of the sacrifice he would make? Selysette insists that Aglavaine shall stay. Without revealing her feelings, Selysette has already made up her mind to withdraw, but not without proving to herself, and to her husband in particular, that her love made her worthy of his, and not without the strength that she will first have to find in the full realization of futility and despair.

Selysette clings to life; to her, the beauty of nature, her affection for people, her love for her husband, are the very reasons for happiness, the basis for her existence; existence is happiness. Aglavaine arrives and her presence makes Selysette feel that her happiness is shattered. Thus life, which for her has no other significance than carefree, playful happiness, has lost its justification. Therefore, any serious threat to her happiness is at the same time a threat to her life. Escape appears to be the only solution. Her intended withdrawal is the outcome of a realization of her weakness and of a feeling of inferiority that destroys her happiness and her desire to live. She is, therefore, toying with the idea of suicide; but in order to strengthen this fatal aspiration, Selysette needs a strong motivation. She needs the proof of defeat, the pain of inflicted injury, and the despair of futility. Without these experiences she cannot muster the strength which could turn a mere desire into a decisive act. In the meantime mere apathy leaves her in a state of uncertainty and vain purposeless search.

Selysette overhears a conversation in the park between Aglavaine and Meleander. They are struggling in vain for a pure and, as they believe, irreproachable love only to find that they are irresistibly drawn to one another and that they are bound to cause suffering to Selysette who they fear is unable to rise to their level of magnanimity. Torn between their desire to keep their love pure and inoffensive and the unavoidable demands of their mutual attraction, they embrace in a moment of despair and anguish. Selysette, in her hiding place, has found the dreaded confirmation of the truth she has been only vaguely suspecting. But she has also recognized, especially in Aglavaine, a moral strength, an awareness of duty, and a pity which awake in her a readiness for self-denial and renunciation.

Selysette is becoming dimly aware of human qualities that her simple and natural selfishness has hidden from her, and that she now recognizes as the clear and pure source of her husband's love and devotion for Aglavaine. She learns that his love is the result of admiration inspired by merit. Selysette experiences pain, but also the effects of that spiritual beauty which commands admiration. Aglavaine's pity and self-denial not only cause Selysette a painfully humiliating feeling of moral inferiority, but they tend, at the same time, to draw her to Aglavaine because of the latter's humane compassion and also because of Selysette's discovery that suffering and a feeling of humane responsibility are at the basis of Aglavaine's self-denial. Selysette's original spontaneous resentment is now tempered by admiration and pity, but the bases of her resentment, the feeling of inferiority and the injury her self-esteem and pride have suffered — these are not diminished; indeed, they are felt more acutely because of her growing realization of Aglavaine's spiritual superiority.

Polyeucte, too, was made to feel inferior to Severus, whose superior merits revived Pauline's love. He, too, was unable to accept his wife's sacrifice by which she would have dutifully given up her love for her Roman hero. He, like Selysette, wished to be loved as he was and for what he was, and not for any merit. Only when he had been made aware that her love was determined by merit and glory alone did he rise, emulating his rival, to heights of self-denial and heroism. He believed it possible to achieve his goal by his death alone; and Selysette, too, will see no other solution. Like Polyeucte, she will have to seek a death which will conceal its true purpose.

Selysette learns intuitively, without ever quite comprehending, that the futility and despair wherein she seeks to find the strength for withdrawing and dying, would mark her as unworthy of Meleander's sorrow and would in no way alter his feelings for Aglavaine. Selysette must learn to equal her rival if she wishes to see Meleander shed the same tears for her as she saw him shed for Aglavaine, when he was moved by her humane self-denial and by despair of their ever being able to live together in the only perfect union they could conceive. Selysette must learn to find a source of happiness in a generous self-denial that will allow Aglavaine and Meleander to be freely happy, and she must also learn to enjoy her own suffering. She must learn to hide her tears, for fear that they may belie her words. She must rise to their level of unselfish love in order to prove herself their equal and to convince them that her happiness lies in theirs. She knows that Aglavaine, with all her spiritual beauty, remains unattainable for Meleander, for fate has caused her to enter his life too late. This lends Aglavaine a fascination for which Selysette would yearn in vain as long as she remained alive. Whereas before, Selysette was seeking the strength to take her own life, she now believes she has found a purpose for her death: it shall regain the love she has lost.

Partly out of pity for Aglavaine, but partly also out of her need to regain Meleander's love, Selysette shows herself not only tolerant, but kind, considerate, and generous too. She knows that Aglavaine is her model. "If I have done anything," she tells her husband, "that you like, it is because I have tried to be like Aglavaine." She must try to prove to them, and particularly to her husband, that she too can rise to her rival's level of magnanimity and spiritual beauty, but she must also try to surpass her by giving up everything — even life — to make them happy.

She would, in her desire to surpass them, like to keep her intended suicide a secret and make it appear to be an accident. But were it nothing but an accident, it could not appear to be a sacrificial act, it could not suggest her morally superior self-denial, her superior spiritual beauty; and were it obviously nothing else than suicide, it would be an act of weakness and despair or an act of cruel vengeance, not likely to win for her Meleander's admiration and love. Just as Polyeucte had to find an acceptable and honorable purpose for his withdrawal, and one that would give proof of his superior virtue, so she, too, must not allow her action to be revealed as the result of an intolerable and humiliating defeat. Above all, she must not allow her suicide to seem like an act of vengeance which had as its purpose the destruction of their happiness by her death.

A significant difference between Polyeucte and Selysette is that he suffers without showing it, whereas she is unable to hide her tears and sadness. In the classical play Polyeucte's suffering is only understood by Pauline; in this essentially romantic play the feelings are apparent and not easily concealed. Selysette has to assure Meleander that her increasing sadness makes her happy, that her tears are not approved by what her mind has come to consider as right.

There is another difference between the two plays: Polyeucte was able to oppose to his suffering his newly acquired faith, and could exchange ephemeral worldly happiness for eternal heavenly bliss, whereas Selysette has no such faith. She does increasingly realize her own selfishness, and this awareness causes her to feel inferior, ashamed, and not worthy of loving admiration. As a result of this realization, she purposely represses her selfishness in order to become worthy, but her efforts to make her mind triumph over her feelings are rarely successful and she appears torn between her half-repressed sadness and an unconvincing pretense of happiness. She knows that her final moral victory can only be assured by her pure and sacrificial death.

Since she can have no recourse to some morally superior cause which could render her death heroic and conceal her ulterior motives, she has to give the impression that her accidental death occurs at a time when she has already reached the height of magnanimity, spiritual beauty, and understanding which would preclude an act of vile revenge or cowardly escape. She must also make sure that her suicide will be clearly enough regarded as such, and that no other motive will be found for it but her kindness, her consideration for the happiness of Meleander, her pity for Aglavaine. In a desperate effort, she hopes to succeed in providing proof that she is worthy of their admiration and in gaining their recognition that she, too, has been able to find joy and happiness in sacrificing herself for those she loved. Her anxious assurances of her happiness, her poorly disguised preparations prior to her fall from the tower of the old lighthouse, her precautions and ill-concealed tears, all tend to have her death understood as it is meant to be understood.

Like Polyeucte, but to a far lesser degree, Selysette came to believe that her intended suicide was an act of renunciation and self-sacrifice. To some extent she actually did become "converted" to that magnanimity which results in self-denial. She did offer Meleander his freedom and proposed to leave, sincerely recognizing Aglavaine's superiority and right to live happily with him. It was Meleander who refused to accept this sacrifice and insisted that he had misjudged her. If one of them was to leave, he maintained, it would have to be Aglavaine. Selysette understood and realized that her husband still regarded her as the weaker, and therefore as the one who could not and should not be made to suffer. While he was thus confirming her feeling of inferiority, Selysette learned that willing endurance of suffering was a mark of moral and spiritual superiority and that her husband, out of pity, was willing to sacrifice his own happiness with Aglavaine rather than accept from his wife a generous sacrifice for which she, who had not the necessary strength, would be made to suffer. Meleander's attitude condemns Selysette to accept his love born of pity, a love that could not restore her happiness, that would perpetuate her humiliation. Only by equalling his sacrifice, by surpassing it, can she assert her dignity and self-esteem. Thus, her self-sacrifice stems from her willing emulation of her rival and from the moral constraint imposed by her husband.

Although the cases of Selysette and Polyeucte seem similar, there is an essential difference between them. His original motivation, viewed objectively, is not the inspiration of religious fervor; but he succeeds in convincing himself that his self-sacrifice is an act of faith. Neither does Selysette's original motivation emanate from a desire to achieve spirtual beauty by her death. But she is unlike Polyeucte in that, with her, only gradually and superficially does this desire become a conscious motive, superimposed on the original one, which was to evoke regret and to withdraw from a humiliating situation in which every desire to go on living was suppressed.

The beliefs of Antigone, of Polyeucte, and of Selysette determine the motives of their self-sacrifice. Antigone has an unshaken faith in the gods and she sacrifices herself to uphold the sanctity of her faith. Polyeucte, whose dignity and pride are hurt and whose vain desire for love drives him to despair, seeks to die, but recognizes that a death which is merely an escape is bound to humiliate him even more. Therefore, he dies for a cause, the very nature of which is bound to restore his dignity and pride and to soothe the pain caused by defeat. Selysette, humiliated, hurt, and driven to despair like Polyeucte, has no worthy cause to fall back upon, no uplifting devotion to save her dignity and self-esteem. She has to learn first on what vertiginous heights human dignity rests; she has to learn to ascend the steep path to spiritual beauty; she has to learn to recognize spiritual salvation in self-sacrifice.

Antigone dies for what she believes in and she accepts her fate. She is challenged by a force that threatens her beliefs and she rises to their defense, fully realizing that her self-sacrifice is the necessary price of her moral victory. The important point is that she does not, ever, doubt the superiority of her beliefs; she stands on firm ground.

Polyeucte and Selysette, however, find themselves faced with a challenge which awakens them to the realization of their inferiority. Antigone finds strength in her beliefs and in the conviction of her righteous superiority; they, on the other hand, must meet the challenge without the power of convictions emanating from values firmly adhered to. There, we find heroism rooted in faith; here, the pathos of insufficiency. There, death is the proof of loyalty to convictions; here, death is escape from defeat. There, death is moral and spiritual victory; here, death is surrender. Nevertheless, faced with death and its implied self-condemnation, Polyeucte and Selysette gain that relative freedom of action and self-realization which the inevitability of doom affords. Defeated as they feel themselves to be by superior worth, spurred by the suffering caused by their defeat, freed from the anguish of self-preservation, they devote their last efforts to self-assertion, to the redemption of their dignity and self-esteem by casting their energy into the very mold which has given shape to their victorious rivals; thus Polyeucte becomes a Christian Severus, and Selysette a sentimental Aglavaine.

Antigone's death is sacrificial because of her free, though painful and sorrowful, self-denial. Her sacrificial death is tragic because of her complete renunciation of life, because of the complete fulfillment of her duty and because of the unavoidable doom to which the fulfillment of her duty leads. Finally, her death is tragic because her motives for self-sacrifice derive from the realization and acceptance of a view of life in which her deeply cherished happiness is subordinated to a value which she accepts as superior. Polyeucte and Selysette sacrifice their lives for a superior value, too; but initially this superior value is merely a pretext and it only gradually develops into the purpose of their self-sacrifice, to the extent to which their "conversion" and their adaptation to the chosen mold is accomplished. Antigone meets the challenge armed with a fixed purpose and her death confirms her adherence to it. Polyeucte and Selysette are forced to develop a purpose to make their death, which is a foregone conclusion, worthy.

The conflict, however, is in all three cases a tragic one, whether it be Antigone's conflict between expediency and conviction or Polyeucte's and Selysette's conflict between a degrading adherence to life and their sense of honor and dignity. As has already been pointed out, they could all choose to live and ignore the challenge. Antigone's conviction and conscience force her to engage her life in the struggle and Polyeucte's and Selysette's sense of honor forces them to an honorable stand. Self-denial, renunciation, self-sacrifice and inevitable doom are the necessary consequences of Antigone's course and they become the necessary consequences of Polyeucte's and Selysette's sense of honor, once they discover their worthy cause.

Polyphème

THE action of Albert Samain's *Polyphème* sheds further light on the dichotomy of causes which lead to self-sacrifice in *Polyeucte* and *Aglavaine and Selysette*. Polyeucte's self-esteem and honor lead to his death as much as his newly embraced faith does. Selysette's vanity and honor lead to her death just as much as her newly acquired sense for Aglavaine's spiritual beauty. Both come to believe in superior motives for the death which, initially, they seek as an escape from an unendurable feeling of inferiority. To save their self-esteem and arouse the esteem of others, they eagerly adopt a worthy cause, the complete devotion to which lends moral justification to what otherwise would be little more than an act of despair.

Like Polyeucte and Selysette, Polyphemus suffers from a feeling of inferiority. Polyeucte's and Selysette's feelings of inferiority are awakened in them when they are confronted by rivals of spiritual superiority; they can therefore strive to emulate their examples and to surpass their virtues. Polyphemus, whose feeling of inferiority stems from his ugliness, has no hope of surpassing his handsome rival in appearance; he is, therefore, trying to rise to a spiritual superiority by a display of kindness and magnanimity. In *Polyphème*, the dichotomy of causes that lead to self-sacrifice is more obvious than in the other two plays; Polyphemus' desire to prove his spiritual superiority does not blend too easily with his feeling of inferiority, to form a single motive for renunciation and self-sacrifice, and his spiritual aspirations do not become crystallized until after his act of renunciation, when he looks back upon it.

The tragic experience of Samain's Polyphemus can be better appreciated if his mode of self-assertion — renunciation and self-sacrifice — is contrasted with those of the Cyclopes of Homer, Ovid, and Theocritus. Unlike Samain's Polyphemus, Homer's Cyclops, the one-eyed giant Polyphemus who devoured six of Odysseus' comrades, is a lawless and heartless monster. He knows his strength and enjoys it, for it allows him to disdain gods and men alike. He loves to satisfy his hunger. Ovid's Polyphemus is not only aware of his great strength, but his self-satisfaction is such that it shields him against all pain. When he finds cause to be jealous of Galatea's love for the shepherd Acis, he readily compares himself with his rival and is delighted with his own appearance:

Surely I know myself; lately I saw my reflection in a clear pool and I liked my features when I saw them. Just look, how big I am! Jupiter himself up there in the sky has no bigger body; for you are always talking of some Jove or other as ruling there. A wealth of hair overhangs my manly face and it shades my shoulders like a grove. And don't think it ugly that my whole body is covered with thick, bristling hair. A tree is ugly without its leaves and a horse is ugly if a thick mane does not clothe his sorrel neck; feathers clothe the birds, and their own wool is becoming to sheep; so a beard and shaggy hair on his body well become a man. True, I have but one eye in the middle of my forehead, but it is as big as a good-sized shield. And what of that? Doesn't the great sun see everything here on earth from his heavens? And the sun has but one eye . . . *

His love for Galatea is merely the desire to possess her, just as he proudly possesses his other riches. He resents his defeat by Acis whom he considers to be inferior to himself. It is the defeat that provokes him, not Galatea's disdain, for, to him, she is merely a desirable object of possession and could be an added proof of his power. As long as no one else can succeed where he himself

* Ovid *Metamorphoses*, trans. Frank Justus Miller (Loeb Classical Library; Harvard University Press, 1929), Vol. II, pp. 287, 289.

is failing, he remains relatively undisturbed. Acis' success, however, does represent a challenge, because it marks for Polyphemus the limits of his power. This is a realization his pride cannot endure and Acis has to pay for it with his life.

An earlier Polyphemus, the one of Theocritus, is actually capable of love. His deep yearning for Galatea is quite sincere. He knows that he is ugly, but he also knows what he is ready to offer for a love that would bring him happiness. He is rich and is willing to buy her love, but he senses that his craving for Galatea's love is futile, that his dreams of happiness may never be realized. Lamentation, brooding, even despair could be the result of so painful a realization, but Theocritus' Polyphemus is not a man of powerful emotions. He could use threats or force, but he prefers to place his trust in the attraction of his wealth. The comforts of life appear so desirable to him that he is unable to believe Galatea can resist their temptation for long. This is the basis for his optimism, for his patience, and for his quick consolation; and if it is not Galatea, other maidens can be found who do appreciate his importance.

As these examples show, Polyphemus has been variously depicted as a monster, as a demigod, or as a rich and confident farmer. As a monster or demigod, he has no real problems. When challenged, he may get hurt, but his strength gives him the confidence to assert himself by force or threats of force. The Polyphemus of Theocritus is more refined; he does not resort to brutal force, primarily because he does not need to, since he knows the alluring power of his wealth. Instead of winning his happiness by force, he buys it. To the Polyphemus of the *Metamorphoses*, or of the *Odyssey*, everything he wants presents a challenge, a test of his strength. Anything he wants to have is of importance, for it may confirm or disprove his faith in his strength and thus his faith in his life and happiness. To the Polyphemus of Theocritus nothing is important, except his wealth. If he wants Galatea for himself and does not succeed, he can still hope that she may change her mind; and if she should not, others can take her place, for no thing or person is very important. His wealth breeds consolation whenever his heart, forgetful of the unimportance of its desires, is gripped by some passing pain.

Without some doubt in one's strength and without any feeling of limitations, there is no struggle. Without adherence to an established set of values that determine the relative importance of the objects of one's desires, there is no discriminating will; and without ascribing to some of these objects a paramount importance, to which one's very existence is subordinate, there is no conviction, no willingness for sacrifice and suffering, no tragic conflict.

In Samain's *Polyphème* there are some traces of Ovidian and Theocritean characterizations, but Samain has made of Polyphemus a heroic character and, in a sense, a tragic character. He has reduced his stature from that of a Cyclops to that of an ordinary man, changing him from a demigod of unbounded self-assurance to a self-conscious person who is troubled by doubts and anxious to assert himself, from a self-centered and self-satisfied giant to a passionate and tender lover. Yet, in the vehemence of his passions, in his outbursts of anger, and in his self-inflicted pain, one recognizes the savage, though tamed, and the primitive, though yoked to an awe-inspiring divine morality.

Polyphemus loves Galatea and is jealous of her love for the shepherd Acis. His first impulse is to kill her, to shatter her against the rocks of the shore. Like Selysette, he feeds his anger by watching their tender love scene; like Selysette, he incites himself against his loved one; but quite unlike Selysette he gathers his strength with the intention of smothering her whom he considers to be the cause of his suffering. Instead, however, he turns his fury against himself, runs into the woods and blinds himself. Finally, he asks Galatea's little brother Lycas to lead him to the sea, and he drowns himself.

It is in his hiding place, while watching the tender love scene between Galatea and Acis, that Polyphemus is faced for the first time with the stark reality of their love, of Galatea's disdain for himself and of Acis' pity. Galatea's true feelings are revealed to him, shattering all his hopes, humiliating his pride, and making a mockery of his love and tenderness. It is at this moment that he raises his clenched fists, that he is going to strike the avenging blow with the same cruelty with which he is known to choke the monsters in the mountains. But he is unable to vent his anger in the way he has intended. He, who was begging for her affection, sees her lavish her love on another; he, who is unable to find happiness in any other way than by making Galatea happy, exclaims in consternation: "Their happiness seizes me with dismay!" He, the strong, the brave, the chivalrous, the worthy, is witnessing his utter defeat: "What strange feeling holds thus back my arms? It is no use wanting . . . I feel that I am unable . . ." He is so astonished and overwhelmed that he feels paralyzed, as in a nightmare, and incapable of recovering from the shock of his crushing experience and the petrifying sight. It is at this point that he runs into the woods and blinds himself.

Polyphemus returns blinded to evoke, no doubt, Galatea's pity, to move her by his suffering and by the sight of his mutilated features. But Galatea is asleep and Lycas keeps a silent watch. Polyphemus does not wish to wake the sleeping maiden and prefers to entrust his confessions to Lycas, on whose affection he can count. Bending over Galatea, Polyphemus whispers: "Do not fear my justice. Sleep without comprehending ever so little my sacrifice. Sleep . . ." He reflects on what has happened and his previous outcry, "their happiness seizes me with dismay!" contrasts significantly with his present interpretation, for he now remembers that he felt "his rage and fury burst" and all that remained was a "great suffering which gave birth to kindness."

What caused his rage and fury to turn into kindness? His irrefutable realization of their love and of his defeat made him aware of what he considered to be treason, but now he believes himself to have discovered the will of destiny in their love and, bowing to the will of the gods, he forgives their treason and goes so far as to plead with the deities which surround his abode:

> Protect forever this sleeping child . . .
> Let her remain ignorant of the evil which was
> atoned by evil:
> Do have for her, do, a small part of my pity!

His sudden awareness of the will of the gods and of Galatea's own ignorance of her treacherous attitude is, then, the source of his kindness and pity now that he is blind, now that the pain of jealousy and the dismay at the sight of their happiness are erased from his memory.

As in the case of Oedipus, the role of the visual image is, once again, confirmed. By blinding himself, Polyphemus could tear away that burning "sight of caresses and of passion from his fore-head." By "exceeding his wretchedness with a single stroke," he can experience the suffering and gain the insight which lead him to pity, to self-denial, and to the belief of having sacrificed him-self to make Galatea happy. No longer tortured by his vision, appeased by suffering, exalted by his pity, his magnanimity, and his sacrifice, Polyphemus discovers the origin of his unendurable feeling of "shame and weakness" in his intended cruelty and he comes to regard his self-blinding — that act of despair — as an act of atonement. Thereby, he proves, to himself at least and to his watchful witness Lycas, his worth, his kindness, his piety, and his high-minded devotion to Galatea. Tears of remorse cause his "strength to return" and an "unknown peace" to fill his heart.

To understand, however, why his "rage and fury burst" and why it is that his defeat and his act of despair are really brought about by an overwhelming feeling of inferiority, which in turn forces him to redeem and assert himself by regaining his lost feel-ing of worth and power, one must remember that Polyphemus, the king of the forests and son of the great goddess of earth, had been confident, certain of his superiority and certain of Galatea's love until, one evening, he saw his ugly features mirrored in the water of a pond. He could not, like Ovid's Polyphemus, see in his features the expression of grandeur, for he was, in spite of his origin, only a man, used to measuring himself against other men. Nor could he find consolation in his riches, like the Polyphemus of Theocritus, for he values love, affection, and esteem above everything else. After the painful discovery of his ugliness his "tender and savage heart" was uneasy. When he compared his own features with those of Acis, his vanity was hurt and his confidence shaken. He could no longer accept for love Galatea's pretense of affection, and he needed proof that it was he whom she preferred. The more his suspicion increased, the more anxious he became to vie with Acis for her love. He had to choose his own means to win Galatea's heart and so he showered her with gifts, he overwhelmed her with the most tender affection and with an unequalled depth of passion. He tried to move her heart by winning her admiration, her gratitude, and her pity. Sacrificing his pride and self-respect, he stooped to the role of a beggar, and it was in the midst of his most desperate efforts at propitiating Galatea that he suffered his defeat.

The strange feeling, which, at the sight of the lovers, caused his avenging arms to sink helplessly, was that of "shame and weakness" which he recognized, but which, after his blinding, he could no longer fathom in its true meaning. This feeling of shame and weakness turned his anger against himself by making him realize his vain folly, the futility of seeking love by winning gratitude and by begging for pity. He despised himself for this shame and weakness and punished himself for his self-inflicted ignominy and for his defeat. Now, however, his pain and suffering cause him to feel self-pity; and his new point of view, whereby he considers his self-mutilation as at once an act of piety, high-minded devotion, pity, and atonement, and his intended suicide as a self-sacrifice, leads him to believe in his heroism and turns his defeat into a moral victory, his feeling of inferiority into a feeling of superiority over his rival and his death into the proof of the courage of his convictions.

Antigone, Polyeucte, and Selysette had to gather their moral strength in the tragic conflict between spiritual aspirations and their will to live, and the tragic of their fate lay in the inevitability of their self-sacrifice if their spiritual aspirations were to be fulfilled. The decisive act in the struggle for the fulfillment was the act of renunciation.

Samain's Polyphemus does not experience any tragic conflict; he does not suffer from a realization of the inevitability of his self-sacrifice, for he is contemplating revenge. He is not tortured by the necessity of living up to spiritual aspirations and, therefore, he is not led to renunciation in order to support and maintain them. His defeat is an unconscious experience. Consciously, he is striving to maintain his superiority by destroying his rival and even Galatea, and he feels hurt, cruelly mistreated, sinfully misled; but he does not admit his feeling of inferiority.

Unconsciously, however, he does feel inferior when he sees himself as Galatea does. In his effort to please her, he cannot help viewing himself with her eyes and, consequently, his behavior depends on what he considers to be her judgment. His unconscious feeling of inferiority is the hidden force which makes his avenging fists slacken and his fury burst; therein is the cause of his defeat, of his anger, and of the pain of which he has to free himself by "exceeding his wretchedness with a single stroke," by self-mutilation. Unable to assert his superiority by revenge, he strives to attain a moral superiority which, in his own eyes, justifies his miscarried attempt at self-assertion by garbing it with generosity, pity, and highminded devotion. Even though this may not assure him Galatea's love and thus his victory, at least it raises his hopes of her gratitude and pity.

The unconsciousness of his defeat deprives the play of a tragic conflict and of tragic renunciation. But in retrospect — and herein lies the distinction of this play — Polyphemus does experience the same urgency to adhere to superior values, the same need to prove his aspirations by self-denial and sacrifice, the same craving for moral self-assertion and for saving his self-esteem as Antigone, Polyeucte, and Selysette. Samain, the lyric poet, makes Polyphemus share their tragic emotions, but as a dramatist he fails to create the tragic conflict.

Conclusion

MARTYRDOM and self-sacrifice are tragic if they emerge from a conflict between authentic worldly and spiritual aspirations. Without such a conflict, without the necessity to measure one's allegiance to an ideal, without an act of renunciation, martyrdom and self-sacrifice are outside the sphere of the tragic. Oedipus, Antigone, Polyeucte, and Selysette, all experience the mental distress of a real renunciation, whereas the distress Polyphemus experiences is over an illusory renunciation. Except for Polyphemus, they could all hold on to the treasured life they lead if conscience, honor, and dignity would let them accept expediency as a norm for their behavior and unworthiness as a personal attribute. The fact that their final decisions prove that they can accept neither expediency nor unworthiness and that they appear, by inner compulsion, forced into upholding their ideals, their honor, and their dignity does not suggest that their renunciation is thereby made easier. Indeed, there is no renunciation possible — a renunciation based on a decision which is free of any exterior compulsion — unless it is the outcome of an evaluation, unless the relative importance of equally appealing, though not equally compelling, values is determined.

Oedipus' renunciation is essentially an act of atonement, Antigone's is essentially an act of obedience. In both instances it is the fulfillment of duty imposed by faith. Loyalty and responsibility tie them to divine laws as they already know them; respectful humility ties them to mysterious laws, which reveal their validity as fate unfolds their disconcerting effects. Life, for both, is a trust.

The renunciation of Polyeucte and Selysette is essentially an outgrowth of defeat, but simultaneously an act of glory, dignity, and self-esteem. They are both aware of the moral strength and the feeling of superiority which emanate from a voluntary renunciation and self-sacrifice. They also feel the liberating effect of defeat and unavoidable doom. Defeated by superior merit and thereby made to feel inferior, they renounce, in emulating their superior rivals, whatever worldly aspirations they still may have and abandon themselves to the necessity of death as a means of restoring their lost distinction by emulating their superior rivals whose chief merit lies in magnanimously renouncing the rights their virtue has acquired.

Polyphemus' defeat is also the effect of a rival's superiority and his renunciation is primarily intended to restore his self-esteem; it is a gesture aimed at achieving the consolation of a feeling of superiority; but it is an illusion, for he is not renouncing happiness, he is merely giving up the hope for a love — and in this he differs from Polyeucte and Selysette — that would have made him happy even though it could only have been prompted by Galatea's pity.

Renunciation imposed by duty or by the desire for glory is the cathartic element of these tragedies. It characterizes man's relation to man in a divine order or in an order in which man's spirit is the seat of his moral nature. In the former order, man is subordinated to the will of a deity and his self-sacrifice is intended to fulfill the firm and inflexible duties imposed by this relationship. In the latter, man is subordinated to spiritual values and his self-sacrifice is intended to confirm his loyal adherence to them.

It may be argued that in Oedipus and in Antigone fear rather than awe is the foundation on which their devotion to the divine law rests, and that in Polyeucte and in Selysette vanity rather than human dignity is the source of their spiritual values.

But it must not be forgotten that their fear or vanity merely represents the human depth from which their spirits rise and that both fear and vanity are overshadowed and even conquered by their loyalty to spiritual values; that loyalty evolves in the distressing conflict between servility to life and aspirations of the spirit, and is proven by the suffering of renunciation, which culminates in self-sacrifice.

> Virtue's ends from Vanity can raise,
> Which seeks no interest, no reward but praise;
> And build on wants, and on defects of mind,
> The joy, the peace, the glory of Mankind.
>
> POPE, *Essay on Man*

INDEX

Index